KW-219-656

Ready made activities for
SUCCESSFUL ACCOUNT MANAGEMENT

The Institute of Management (IM) is at the forefront of management development and best management practice. The Institute embraces all levels of management from students to chief executives. It provides a unique portfolio of services for all managers, enabling them to develop skills and achieve management excellence. If you would like to hear more about the benefits of membership, please write to Department P, Institute of Management, Cottingham Road, Corby NN17 1TT. This series is commissioned by the Institute of Management Foundation.

Ready made activities for SUCCESSFUL ACCOUNT MANAGEMENT

Patrick Forsyth

the Institute of Management

FOUNDATION

PITMAN PUBLISHING

PITMAN PUBLISHING
128 Long Acre, London WC2E 9AN

A Division of Longman Group UK Limited

First published in Great Britain 1994

© Patrick Forsyth 1994

British Library Cataloguing in Publication Data
A CIP catalogue record for this book can be obtained from the British Library.

ISBN 0 273 61178 X

All rights reserved; no part of this publication may be reproduced, stored
in a retrieval system, or transmitted in any form or by any means, electronic,
mechanical, photocopying, recording, or otherwise without either the prior
written permission of the Publishers or a licence permitting restricted copying
in the United Kingdom issued by the Copyright Licensing Agency Ltd,
90 Tottenham Court Road, London W1P 9HE. This book may not be lent,
resold, hired out or otherwise disposed of by way of trade in any form
of binding or cover other than that in which it is published, without the
prior consent of the Publishers.

10 9 8 7 6 5 4 3 2 1

Typeset by PanTek Arts, Maidstone, Kent.
Printed and bound in Great Britain by Clays Ltd, St Ives plc.

The Publishers' policy is to use paper manufactured from sustainable forests.

Contents

Buyers Are a Tough Lot

It is any buyer's job to get the best possible deal for his company. That is what they are paid for, they are not actually on the salesmen's side, and will attempt to get the better of them in every way, especially on discounts.

This is well illustrated by the apocryphal story of the fairground strongman. During his act he took an orange, put it in the crook of his arm and bending his arm squeezed the juice out. He then challenged the audience, offering £10 to anyone able to squeeze out another drop.

After many had tried unsuccessfully, one apparently unlikely candidate came forward, he squeezed and squeezed and finally out came a couple more drops. The strongman was amazed, and, seeking to explain how this was possible, asked as he paid out the £10 what the man did for a living. 'I am a buyer with Ford Motor Company', he replied.

Buyers are not really like this; they are worse.

from *Everything You need to Know about Marketing*
by Patrick Forsyth (Kogan Page)

Foreword

If there is one thing most managers have in common, it is pressure on their time. In an increasingly hectic and competitive world, where change is the order of the day, there is rarely time for everything that needs to be done and setting the right priorities is a p rerequisite of success. Training can all too often take a back seat. It is acknowledged as an archetypal 'good thing', yet too often ends up neglected. So anying that makes it easier to implement and thus more certain to occur is all to the good.

This volume, in a series under the title *Ready Made Activities*, is designed to do exactly that, providing a practical approach to developing the essential sales skills which are so crucial to commercial success in a competitive environment.

It is designed to set out guidelines to conducting a complete training session on account management and development. It is self-standing, though it can also act as a 'part two' to my volume on face-to-face selling skills *Ready Made Activities for Selling Skills*. It is presented in the form of a training plan that is:

● **prescribed**, that is the core content can be followed stage by stage, saving time in preparation, and ensuring that the coverage necessary to present the techniques and approaches fundamental to sales success is presented thoroughly

● **participative**, including clear information about how involvement can be included in a way that will improve the learning that the session will prompt

● **flexible**, arranged so that it can easily accommodate addditional elements, particularly those designed to produce a focus on the individual product or service with which participants are involved and any other specifics of the organisation, industry or customers which make every sales situation unique

● **practical**, including all the information necessary to conduct the session – with suggestions regarding examples, visuals and the training techniques that are necessary to make it successful

all in a style which provides an appropriate and useful basis for **both line managers and those with little or no traning or presentational experience to work from, as well as an aid to training specialists, perhaps especially those without a sales training background.**

After the introduction, a clear **how to use this material** section sets out the way in which material is presented and how it can be used. Thereafter the material follows the sequence of the training session it describes, with support material following for those who need additional guidance on the presentation of the material.

Having been involved in marketing, sales and communication skills training in a variety of forms for some twenty years I am pleased to be involved in this new series. Pitman has developed an enviable reputation for the quality of their material in recent years, and having contributed to their Financial Times series (*Marketing Professional Services*) and their Institute of Management series (*Marketing for Non-marketing Managers* and *First Things First*) I was pleased to work with them again. This new volume, together with the early one on face-to-face skills, now provides comprehensive coverage of the sales process: including finding and approaching prospects, selling to them initially and then creating and building on a relationship that will allow and encourage repeat and additional business on a regular basis.

Selling, in all aspects, is a vital component of an organisation's marketing strategy, and must play its part strongly and effectively if the results achieved by the totality of that effort are to meet the objectives set. Certainly initial success must be followed up in the right way if the initiative is not to be lost. If this material contributes to that process for those using it then it will serve a useful purpose.

Patrick Forsyth
Toutchstone Training & Consultancy
17 Clocktower Mews
London N1 7BB

Acknowledgements

I have managed accounts, and developed them too; some successfully. This in selling a range of products and services from books to export assistance. Account managment remains an important activity for me in my own business. But I never set out to be a trainer. My route to it was through marketing. The marketing of training products, seminars, conferences and publications put me in touch with the world of consultancy and, having joined a consulting firm in a marketing role, I was then encouraged to become involved in client work. Much of my early time as a consultant was spent with the Marketing Improvements Group plc. During that time I wrote a number of books, drawing in part on company material. Some text and diagrams from that material are included – reproduced or adapted – in this title, and I would like to acknowledge that company's permission to do this here.

So, any ability I may have now to set out this sort of material is the result of some twenty years work with a variety of clients as consultant and trainer. The experience I have gained from this, and the suggestions and guidance I have received – and continue to receive – from consultancy colleagues and associates along the way is simply invaluable. So often it is the people whose time is most valuable who are most generous with it in assisting others. Thanks to them all therefore; and to the participants on the many sales courses I have run over the years, and from whose participation and comments I have learned so much.

Writing, a more recent part of my portfolio of activities, necessitates pulling together and presenting from this experience what might best be described as 'best current practice'. What is presented here is not, I am sure, the only way of viewing the sales processes reviewed, but it is one that has been field tested through the many courses and seminars I and my colleagues have conducted for sales people in the past. I hope that by writing about account management in this way, I will not cease to number it amongst the topics I deal with on courses I conduct for organisations in a variety of industries and countries each year. Though I certainly hope it will enable a number of people to do their own thing and get as much satisfaction from it as I have so often had from training.

Two other mentions: first, some of the material on training techniques in Section 3 is adapted from my earlier book *Running an Effective Training Session* (1994: paperback edition) and I am grateful to Gower Publishing for permission to do this. That book, dare I say, might well provide a useful and practical additional reference for those readers using this publication who have no substantial training background or experience (a totally biased recommendation; but if a book about selling cannot contain an unashamed plug, what can?). Secondly, this book is one of a series. When I wrote the first volume on face-to-face selling skills I liaised with Shelia Cane, a consultant with whom I work occasionally on an associate basis, who was concurrently busy writing the companion volume on negotiating skills. This was not only useful in ensuring we adopted we adopted a common approach, but provided a sounding board. As we were both asked to contribute further to the series, this contact continued and thanks are due again for the constructive help I received throughout.

P.F.

1

INTRODUCTION

No one can manage an account until they have one. Selling – the process – covers a wide span of skills, techniques and tasks. It involves the key skills of persuasive communication, and these have to be directed at both new and existing customers, from the moment of initial contact through to the maintenance of long-term business relationships. Account management is thus at the heart of a broader process, a key set of approaches without which long-term business potential cannot be realised. Here it is defined as starting from the need to prospect and includes key tasks to create positive sales productivity.

By way of background we start with some thoughts about the sales process overall (necessarily reiterating thoughts expressed in *Ready Made Training Activities for Sales Skills*) before focusing exclusively on account management. Selling is not only important, it is not so easy as some imagine; to be successful every aspect of it demands a professional approach.

The role of the sales process

If bringing in the business was easy, we would all be rich, and this publication would be of little value. It is however the very reverse of easy. Markets of all sorts are increasingly competitive, customers are increasingly fickle and Emerson's old saying about producing a better mousetrap has been updated by Ed Johnson:

> 'They say if you build a better mousetrap than your
> neighbour, people are going to come running. They
> are like hell! It's marketing that makes the difference.'

and makes good sense. So, marketing – simplistically defined as the process which sets out to bring in the business (having first had something to say about the product or service to be sold) – is the order of the day. Few, if any, companies leave the business generation process to chance, a whole panoply of techniques are routinely used to increase the chances of success. And even that may not be sufficient. Promotional techniques need to be creatively applied and their effectiveness will also be dependent on how appropriately they are targeted at those, who in turn must be well identified, who are genuine prospects for whatever is being supplied.

The mix of promotional techniques includes methods which are different from each other in the way they work. Figure I.1 shows the main techniques and illustrates how they operate in separate ways in terms of their relationship to the customer. Some, such as much public relations activity, acting as

```
┌─────────────────────────────────────────────────┐
│              ┌──────────────────────┐            │
│              │  PUBLIC RELATIONS    │            │
│              ├──────────────────────┤            │
│              │    ADVERTISING       │            │
│              ├──────────────────────┤            │
│              │    DIRECT MAIL       │            │
│              ├──────────────────────┤            │
│              │  SALES PROMOTION     │            │
│              ├──────────────────────┤            │
│              │     SELLING          │            │
│              └──────────────────────┘            │
│                                                  │
│                      CUSTOMER                    │
└─────────────────────────────────────────────────┘
```

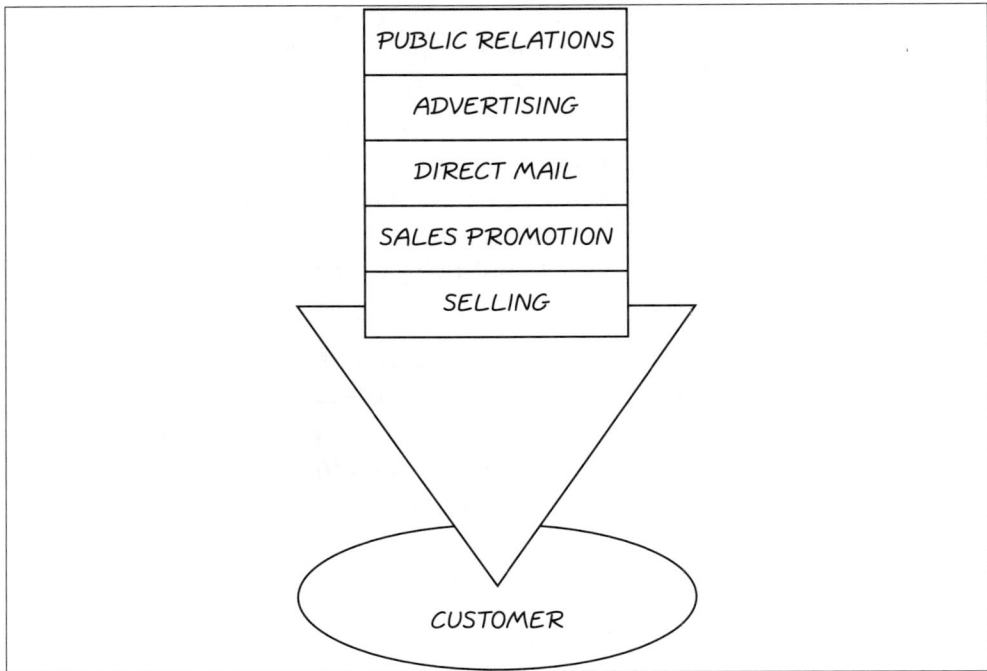

Figure I.1 The mix of persuasive communications

much as anything to create a background image that acts as a foundation for other techniques to build on. Others only work by focusing more closely on the customer. All are important. In some industries, and at some times, one may be more important than another, but rarely is there any one 'magic formula' that bring in the business, a mix is more usually necessary. But one technique is, if not more important, then different in nature and forms the final link between suppliers and customers. That is selling.

This is the only personal, two way, and often one to one, communication in the mix. For many organisations the other promotional tactics create the awareness and interest, but only selling can convert that view into the buying actions that bring in the revenue and thus profit. There is more to selling than may sometimes meet the eye. Its role and objectives are broad. It creates orders, or should do, but it may also need to be instrumental in creating relationships, building loyalty and maintaining and developing business in the longer term.

There is another factor too that is important. Selling, like other promotional activity, must not only spark interest, it must differentiate, and differentiate powerfully, between a particular supplier and competition. Many, perhaps most, products and services have taken on the characteristics of commodities. It is often difficult for potential customers to differentiate between competing cars, computers, caterers or copiers; or at least to do so on any truly objective basis. Technical specifications, and often price, are increasingly similar. Differences will certainly exist, not least in image, service, and amongst the people in the competing organisations. Selling must, as part of its role, highlight such differences and provide solid grounds on which customers can base their choice of one supplier rather than another.

This is, however, to understate the case. Selling, and the sales'people who undertake the task, *must themselves be part of that difference*. They must, by the way they go about their work, contribute to the likelihood of their customers wanting to do business with them rather than someone else. Their role is therefore not just important, it is crucial. All the influences deployed to persuade potential customers to do business operate cumulatively. They progressively build up the level of awareness, interest, understanding and trust that must reach a particular level before customers feel they have weighed up the situation and buying action is then taken. In a competitive world every element that contributes in this way may be significant and the line between a customer being persuaded, or not, may be a fine one. Many throughout the organisation play their part in bringing in the business, but the sales people are in a prime position to ensure that their individual input is significant and, as a result, creates a volume of business that will see the organisation survive and prosper.

It has been said that nothing happens until someone sells something, and commercially at least this may well be true. But selling does not achieve its aims by magic any more than any other marketing technique. There is rarely any such thing as the so called 'born salesman', and going through the motions is never going to bring the right returns however good the product or service involved. Selling must utilise the available techniques and approaches effectively if it is to maximise its success, and this does not just happen. Further, selling in the markets of the nineties, is a fragile process.

As was said earlier, the line between the customer agreeing to buy or not may well be very fine. Similarly things the sales person does which influence whether the customer ends up on one side of the line rather than the other, may be small, indeed may seem insignificant. One word used rather than another. One segment of the sales presentation that is less than clear, that prompts too many questions or seems just that small amount less credible and the effect of what is being done is diluted just enough to weaken the case irretrievably. Of course, the positive side of this is true also. One small difference, one added gesture can work to swing the sale and prompt an order. All this puts a considerable onus on the sales person to make what they do very precise, yet at the same time it must remain a fluid, fluent two-way conversation that gives the customer what they want.

Account management

Success in selling is not, however, only a matter of conducting just the right kind of sales meeting. Selling, as has been said, is a process. It necessitates a number of approaches that must be taken seriously, applied systematically and deployed with the same sort of precision that makes techniques work effectively during a meeting. This requires knowledge and discipline; many a sales person is instinctively happier out in the field 'face to face' than they are thinking through the management of their customer portfolio.

Yet selling is, quite obviously, a numbers game. No one sells successfully to every contact. And success may well be dependent on successful prospecting to create the right number of initial contacts of which a proportion will produce business. Which do so and how certainly is dependent on many factors, not least talking to the best prospects in the first place. Sales people may typically spend only ten to twenty per cent of their working time face to face with customers (not because they are idle, but because there are a variety of other things that take time, particularly travelling). So productivity at the level of organising priorities amongst customers and contacts and of balancing the various tasks – from prospecting to maintaining relationships – is vital.

All sales people need to understand and be able to use the core techniques of persuasion, but this is not sufficient on its own. The topics reviewed here are as vital as such matters as selling the benefits. All that is involved in selling must be deployed literally customer by customer, meeting by meeting, day by day. Standard approaches, applied as it were by rote, have no place in the present market. While there are no magic formulae, there is a route likely to improve results.

Increasing the chances of success

One factor can set sales people apart from those of competitors. Training makes the difference. If there is one factor that does mark out the more successful sales people from their less successful peers, it is an understanding of what makes them successful. This allows them to deploy techniques consciously, but always appropriately, to ensure they have the desired effect. Experience will clearly help cultivate this ability, but it is not guaranteed to do so. Training can accelerate experience, and effective training can certainly contribute to ensuring the ability to operate in a way that suits the market and brings in good results. But training does not just happen any more than orders do. Hence this manual, the intention of which is to ensure that training in this area is made just a little easier and thus more likely to take place.

It takes a practical view, in part behavioural, but also technique-driven. Above all, it is intended to help sales people go about their job with a heightened awareness that will allow them to deploy the right techniques throughout this important aspect of the sales process. It is also intended to help them focus on things from the customer's point of view, because only an approach which respects the customer, and which avoids being patronising or pushy, will end with them wanting to do business with the sales person concerned and seeing them as professional. The best, and perhaps the simplest definition of selling I know is that it is 'helping people to buy'. Its apparent simplicity belies the way it summarises so much of what makes selling successful. This manual is concerned to help you help your sales people to practise such an approach, and to set out clear guidelines to allow you to take them through the core skills and give them a foundation upon which to manage their customers from first contact to lasting business relationship.

The next two sections set out who the material is designed to be used by and the session run for, and exactly how to use the training plan set out in the next chapter.

WHO CAN BEST USE THIS MANUAL

It is difficult to make any material such as this all things to all people. Sales technique *does* need to be applied differently depending on what is being sold to whom. So here the material does have a particular focus, and the format is designed to allow the resulting training session to be still more accurately directed towards your own business.

The emphasis is on the selling of products and services 'business-to-business', rather than the sale of FMCG (Fast-moving consumer goods) through retail channels. The examples chosen as illustrations are simple and easy to relate to, and the material allows a strong link to be made between the general principles and the specific situation within an individual organisation, and the detail of the actual product or service being sold.

The topic

The topic covers a series of issues under the general heading of account management, from prospecting to continuing contact and development. It does not go back into the core face-to-face selling skills (which are covered in the companion volume), though certain specifics have a direct relationship with such skills. Nor does it go further into ancillary skills, such as negotiation (though this is also covered in another volume in the series). It is self-contained and covers its chosen topic so as to provide a complete review.

The ideal participants

The content is designed to act as source material for a session directed at salesmen. This is becoming an unacceptable word in some circles, so I will elaborate. Salesperson may be politically correct, but it describes a category that is too wide for present purposes, including for instance retail staff. Sales representative is old fashioned, both as a word and in concept; there is much more to the job in the nineties than it implies. Perhaps we may settle for 'field sales person' as what it lacks in elegance it makes up for in descriptiveness. If your sales team work externally, calling on buyers (whoever that may be in your business) whether once or in a way that leads, or is designed so to do, to a continuing business relationship then this material will enable you to conduct a training session suitable for them.

It is, in fact, the job and its attendant tasks that matter. It may carry the title of salesman, sales engineer, sales consultant, account (or territory) manager or many more. It may be that the sales people are also the 'production' resource, as in the kind of business where, say, designers or consultants both bring in the business and do the resulting work. Providing their job, or a major part of it is selling the basis of the session will be right. With minimal adjustment it can be directed to new field sales staff, those not so new but with no, or little, formal training, or those with more experience as a refresher.

The ideal 'leader'

The nature of the material makes it suitable for two broad groups of people:

• **managers** in some sort of line or staff role which makes it logical for them to take responsibility for, and undertake, this sort of training. This may mean the sales manager or area manager with relation to their local team or some other middle manager; or it might be a director or general management person in a smaller company, or even a senior sales team member asked to take on this role.

For these the material offers complete guidance, and flexibility if required. It will save preparation time and make the conduct of a successful session more certain. It offers guidance on the how of running (e.g. presentation techniques) as well as structure and coverage.

● **trainers**, who can either simply use it as a time saver (or to cross-check thinking with another source) for the more experienced, or to fill in gaps for those less experienced or without links with the sales function.

Whichever category you fall into, and experience shows that in many companies it is non-trainers who are increasingly becoming involved in this kind of exercise, the material is designed to be of practical help in improving sales effectiveness and thus sales results.

HOW TO USE THIS MATERIAL

This material is designed to be self-explanatory and to minimise preparation time. Clearly the user will need to read the material in its entirety before embarking on conducting a training session, and you may also want to make additional notes to have with you as you run the session. However, the material follows the sequence of the session it describes and is arranged so that its various elements stand out as signposts to the effective conduct of the session. Even the typeface is chosen so that everything is presented in a size that may be comfortably read while standing in front of a group session.

As an overall approach it is suggested that you:

● complete reading this section first
● read through the total training plan
● check whether how you will conduct the session will be aided by referring to the later material providing information about training techniques, and referring to any elements you feel will be useful
● decide which elements of the programme you will use
● add any necessary notes you will need to have in front of you
● relate what you want to do to the nature of the group and the numbers who will attend, so that for instance participative elements will fit in
● check and arrange the equipment and environmental factors (a checklist to assist this process completes this section)

then you will be in a position to make final arrangements and conduct the session.

THE ELEMENTS OF THE MATERIAL

As you read on you will notice that the material includes the following elements which are commented on in turn:

Main content

The main thread of the material in terms of suggested running instructions for the leader, and detail of the coverage to be presented, appears sequentially. All main headings are **in large bold type** to facilitate rapid, easy reference as you conduct the session. All key instructional words:

- introduce
- explain
- discuss
- ask

- emphasise
- make a note
- stress
- summarise

appear in **bold type** to make sure they stand out. Further bold type is used within the text **to provide additional emphasis** and guide the eye to the key parts of the text. In addition to this text, clearly indicated **background notes** appear in boxed pages to give you more detail of the topic under review. This information intentionally goes a little beyond the content indicated in the running guidelines, both to provide background and to allow you to base what you finally present on whatever is most appropriate for the group. This aspect of the content is addressed to those doing the selling, i.e. as you will need to put it over. Once you have read and digested this additional information you may well wish to use it more as general background information rather than follow it slavishly, using the remaining, main, text as the core skeleton that will enable you to direct the session.

Examples

There is a need in any training to exemplify points made to explain, maintain interest and make lessons relate to the actual job to be done by the participant. Examples appear progressively through the text – as do spaces where you may wish to add examples relating to your own organisation and especially to the product or service which you supply. This provides a key opportunity to tailor the material more specifically to your own circumstances.

Symbols

Additional elements within the text are all flagged by appropriate symbols in the margin, again so that you can focus on all the different elements easily and quicky as you go through the total material. These include the following:

✎ Visuals

Certain points are worth showing as well as saying (repetition and seeing as well as hearing are proven aids to learning). Suggestions as to which points are dealt with in this way appear throughout the text. The simplest way of implementing these is to write up material on a flipchart, or table-top presenter. This can be done as the session progresses or made ready in advance and simply turned through as you go.

Of course, if other methods are available, for instance an overhead projector, such material can be prepared as slides or written as you proceed using an acetate roll or sheets (see page 114).

Two forms of suggestion are made:

- a general suggestion made within the text to write something
- specific suggestions shown in the form that might result on flipchart

You can, of course, list more than is suggested and should look particularly for more visual images (within your artistic ability if you are using the flipchart or preprepared).

☞ Participation

Certain topics lend themselves to discussion or involvement, indeed any meeting such as is discussed here needs to include participation to maintain interest, improve learning and the link between the material covered and implementation. Clear suggestions appear at appropriate points setting out participative elements that can be included – whether they are the simple asking of a question, brief discussion or something more involved such as an exercise or role playing.

Note: with an interactive skill such as selling, **role playing** is a well proven way of improving awareness and bridging the gap between training and real life and real prospects and customers. It is specifically suggested, towards the end of the training plan, that each participant has an opportunity to undertake a role play situation. Basic details of how to set this up are given in context and more information about how to make role play effective appears later (see page 126).

The flexibility of the material

Whatever the configuration of your ideal training session, it may rarely be possible to proceed with exactly this as your structure. Some compromise is nearly always involved, especially regarding time and money. Thus it is not always possible to spend as long on things, or include as much participation, as you might wish. In addition, everyone's priorities vary. What may be important in one organisation may be less so in another, and taking more time over one element or topic may necessitate taking less over another.

The material is designed to be flexible. While it provides a comprehensive skeleton, the format allows additional tailoring towards the needs of a specific group – for instance by adding examples as referred to above. To facilitate this process still further, certain elements of the programme may be regarded as **options**, that is they may be omitted without disrupting the flow of the main thread of the content. This allows the material to be condensed somewhat, or for more tailoring (more added examples or participation, for example) to take place without extending the overall time the training takes.

Note: at key break points throughout the material there is space for you to note timings. The precise timings will be conditioned by:

- the number attending
- the exact programme conducted
- the amount of planned, and reactive, participation
- the role play element

and, to some extent, by the experience of the presenter.

Given manageable numbers, certainly 8–12, it should be possible to go through the suggested main content in one day, with the role play adding on a pro rata basis. If necessary or desirable you may want to schedule a longer, or shorter, session and could split the coverage in other ways (for example, a series of evening sessions).

Make the material your own

Now, with this organisation in mind you can proceed to the main training plan. Remember it is *your* session we are talking about, so one final point: as has been made clear, this book is designed to be a working tool. It is unlikely to do as good a job as is possible unless you overcome the natural reluctance which most people have to write in a book. It is designed for it; no one will mind. So do add your own notes and examples where appropriate and consider highlighting – in a second colour or with a fluorescent highlighting pen – to indicate the emphasis *you* want and make key points stand out. If you use it to provide not simply guidance to conducting the session, but guidance to conducting *your* session, it will be that much more useful and your participants will find what you put over that much more helpful to their work in the field.

Note: if you aim, or might, conduct workshops from this material more than once then some additional note-taking may well be useful. This need results from the participative nature of any training. For example, if you make a point, then quote an example and then ask for thoughts about additional examples, you may well find that some good examples are volunteered. If so, some or all of these may be worth recording to use as part of the next presentation. In other words your annotated material will become more valuable with use.

2

THE TRAINING WORKSHOP

H ere, in the main section of this book, the plan for conducting the workshop is laid out session by session. If you have read the explanatory sections in Section 1 you will recognise the various elements as they appear, and will find that the guidelines on *how* to proceed through the session alternate with the content (primarily in the **background notes**) that needs to put over.

Once you have been through this section, then personalise it to whatever degree you feel useful, a process that may include skipping some elements as well as adding, you should be able to conduct the session with these pages, and any visuals you decide to prepare, in front of you to act as the prime element of your 'lecture/running notes'.

Programme objectives

These are defined as to assist participants to:

- locate 'suspects' and decide which are worth actively pursuing as prospects
- make effective contact – by letter or telephone (or both) – with prospects to secure a meeting
- plan for the meeting (and all that may entail) to maximise effectiveness
- assign priorities and plan follow through action, short term and longer term to create ongoing and developing relationships

Programme structure

Before going in to the detail of the session, it may be useful to get the overall 'shape' of it in mind. The flow chart that follows sets out the various stages and elements graphically, and is designed to help you to keep the entirety of the session in mind throughout the process, so that the individual elements are clearly in context.

This 'workshop map' is arranged so that you can add any notes and details you wish, and the elements of the resulting chart might form a useful basis for a visual for use as the group session progresses.

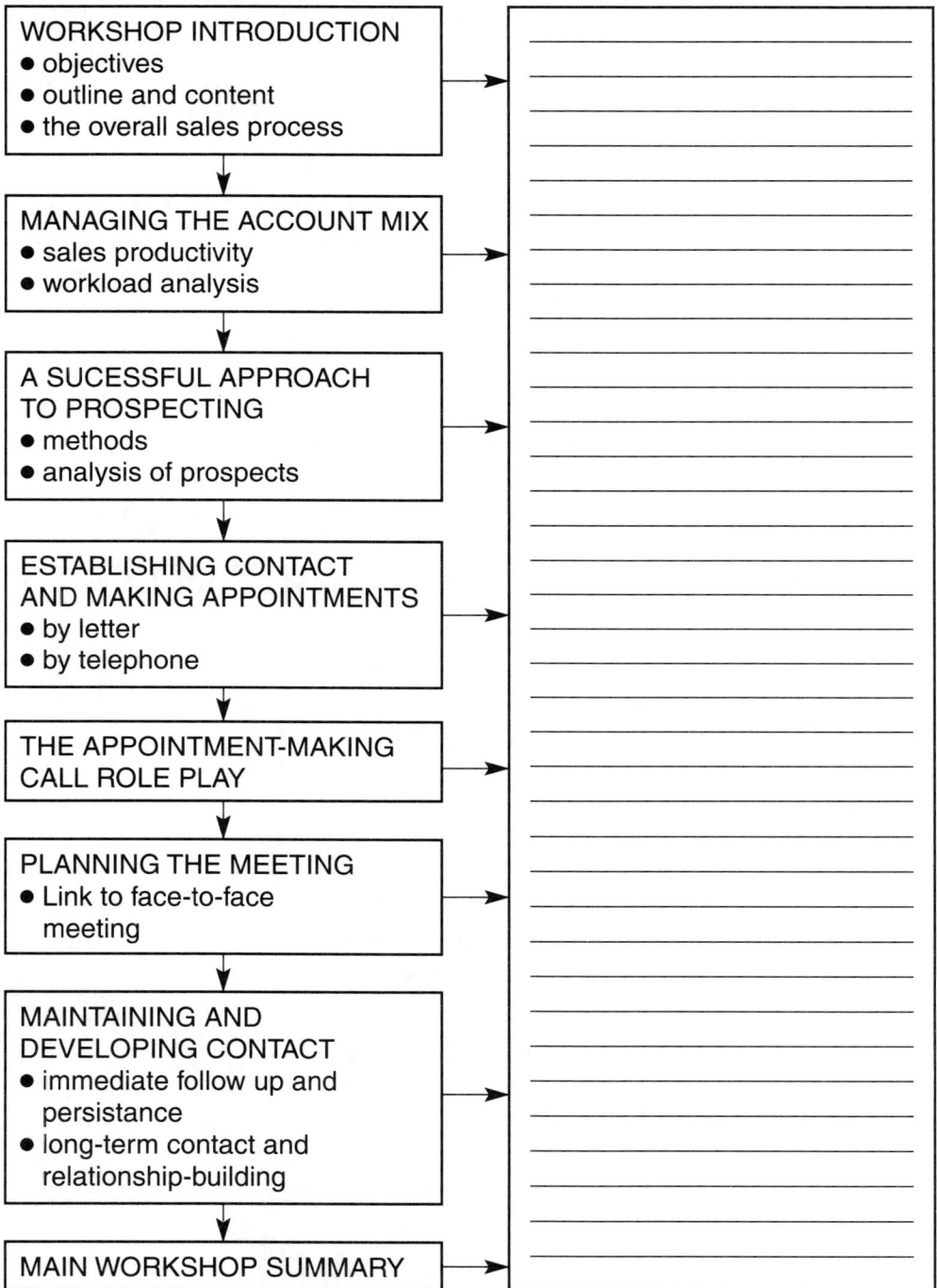

WORKSHOP MAP

WORKSHOP INTRODUCTION
- objectives
- outline and content
- the overall sales process

MANAGING THE ACCOUNT MIX
- sales productivity
- workload analysis

A SUCESSFUL APPROACH TO PROSPECTING
- methods
- analysis of prospects

ESTABLISHING CONTACT AND MAKING APPOINTMENTS
- by letter
- by telephone

THE APPOINTMENT-MAKING CALL ROLE PLAY

PLANNING THE MEETING
- Link to face-to-face meeting

MAINTAINING AND DEVELOPING CONTACT
- immediate follow up and persistance
- long-term contact and relationship-building

MAIN WORKSHOP SUMMARY

Session 1
....
Overall introduction

START TIME:

Introduce yourself and let course participants introduce themselves if they do not already know each other.

THE OBJECTIVES

Before making clear the course objectives:

Explain any topical factors – internal or external – which make the course important now.

For example:

- new market opportunities to be explored
- attrition rate of existing customers has changed
- decision taken to increase geographical coverage
- growth plans demand higher old/new customer ratio etc.

Make a note of any specific topical factors you want to mention:

_____

_____

_____

_____

_____

_____

Explain the objectives (these are set out on the first page of this section).

You may want to list these on the flipchart (or even leave them visibly at the front throughout the session).

Emphasise the practical nature of the programme.

Explain the coverage and link to the timetable (and any necessary administrative details – breaks, meals, loos etc.).

Emphasise that the whole process involved is a *necessary* preliminary to being able to sell face to face (however much of a chore it seems).

Make a note of any other points you may wish to include to make the workshop as relevant as possible:

_____

_____

_____

_____

_____

_____

Ask for any questions from the group before proceeding.

TIME:

BACKGROUND NOTES

Introduction

Selling is a complex process. It is dependent on a number of factors, the techniques used, the manner in which they are deployed and, not least, the rapport and relationship built up between salesperson and customer.

And, it is never easy. Indeed competitive times make it more difficult, and a dynamic market means that approaches are always needed to change and the process of seeking after the 'best approach' never ends.

Every aspect of selling poses its own problems, and presents its own opportunities. Traditionally most training looks at selling from the point of view of the face-to-face relationship. This is clearly the key. There is a danger, however, that this assumes that all customer relationships already exist, and of course they do not. New customers have to be sought out constantly both to build the business and, quite possibly, to replace those who go elsewhere or become inappropriate in some way for the future. Thereafter a relationship has to be established and managed to develop business in the long term.

This process demands a range of actions and skills. You have to decide who to approach (and who not to), how to set up and organise the initial approaches that turn suspects into prospects and, ultimately, new customers; and how to go about the whole process with an eye on both productivity and profitability to maintain and develop future relationships and busines.

The sales process

Consider the sales process as a whole before turning to the detail of the elements just outlined. We live in dynamic times. Change is continuous and the pace of change is ever increasing.

In selling the most important aspects of this are evident in

● greater competitiveness; a greater number of competitors and more professional competitive activities in both marketing overall, and in selling specifically

● more professionalism amongst buyers who are better able to make assessments of products or services, make comparisons and act on what they believe are considered decisions

Customers themselves are under pressure from this competitiveness. Their need for service, technical excellence, the specification being met, delivery on time, advice, support and so on take their form from their particular circumstances; and the salesperson must relate to these circumstances, appropriately and acceptably.

In selling today you must understand sales techniques, and be able to deploy them in a more prepared and more conscious professional approach to selling, than ever before. There is no doubt that today's effective salespeople:

● use structure as a foundation for applying selling skills

● think about what they do

● tailor their approach customer by customer, meeting by meeting

● 'fine-tune' constantly

And, this means that all the preliminary activity that takes place *before* face-to-face contact is vital. Quite simply, unless such activity is executed effectively the face-to-face impact will be diluted, and in extreme cases will not occur. Prospects will not agree to be seen.

Now, what most sales people like best about their job are the core elements. The face-to-face contact with customers, the relationships cultivated and the orders thus obtained. To be honest, the preliminary aspects can be a chore. Prospecting, research and so on, take time; time that could be spent with customers. That is bad enough, but other tasks are psychologically difficult – cold selling on the telephone for one.

If you are saying 'quite right' to yourself about this, remember two points:

● because salespeople commonly feel like this, there is a tendency to skimp these tasks and prevailing standards are, as a result, lower than in some other aspects of the sales task

● if prevailing standards are low, then it presents an immediate opportunity for those who get it right

Some of the aspects of selling reviewed hereafter are not, specifically, the most exciting aspects of the job. No matter, they do provide a real opportunity to create an 'edge' in the market, which, if your face-to-face skills are already good, can create a powerful combination.

With that in mind let us turn to the first stage of these preliminary processes.

Session 2

· ·

Managing the account mix

START TIME:

Explain the rationale and concept of the topic.

Stress the importance of the topic as a foundation to success in face-to-face selling and thus to achieving sales targets.

Introduce the concept of 'sales productivity', a key element of this session.

Ask what people think it costs to make a sales visit. (If you do not know, work it out in advance, remembering to include training, recruitment, administration and management costs as well as salary, cars, commission and expense.)

Write the answers on the flipchart.

Emphasise (or add) the correct figure, the size of which may surprise everyone. Moral: calls have to be made cost effective; productivity is important in the sales role.

Next, proceed to investigate sales productivity further using two exercises. Both of these are marked as **options**, though both are worthwhile if time allows. Sufficient detail is shown to complete them, you may prefer however to amend these details to give you something more tailored to your own organisation.

Sales productivity: Exercise 1

Explain what people need to do (a prepared handout may simplify this) and **ask** for the calculation to be made. Note and comment on the answer; the number of calls and the need to make the best of all of them is normally clear.

Exercise 1
Sales productivity

The left-column below gives an example of available sales time, in terms of days and calls.

Complete the right-hand column for your own situation (using intelligent guesses for any areas where you are unclear and cannot check).

Days in the year		365	365
Less Holidays	21		
Weekends	104		
Sickness (av.)	3		___
		128	
		233	
Less • sales meetings	4		
• appraisal	1		
• administration	25		
• training	3		
• other			
	___	33	___
		200	___

Average calls per
day = 4 200 × 4 =

Number of calls made
per year 800

Average calls per
day = ___ ×

Number of calls
per year is _____

Sales productivity: Exercise 2

This reinforces the productivity point and will get people thinking in workload analysis terms.

Note that in both cases the total number calls must include any required allowance for prospecting. **Stress** the thinking that any imbalance should prompt.

Exercise 2
Workload analysis

To investigate how the total annual number of calls is utilised and see whether workload and capacity are balanced:

● Count the number of existing and potential customers it is intended to visit during the year.

● Assign to each customer a call frequency – the number of calls it is believed will be sufficient to gain or keep the identified business in the account.

● Calculate the annual number of working days in the field – excluding holidays, sales meetings, training courses, exhibitions, etc. (done in Exercise 1).

● Calculate the average number of calls made on each day in the field.

● Substitute the above figures in the formula:

$$\text{Workload} = \frac{\text{No. of customers/potential customer} \times \text{annual call frequency}}{\text{Average daily call rate} \times \text{no. of working days per year}}$$

The perfect workload should be 1.00. That is to say, the number of calls we intend to make should balance with the number of calls we **can** make. However, since we are not dealing with very precise data there is little cause for concern if the workload varies between 0.90 and 1.10.

If this calculation shows the workload to be too heavy, the following question should be reconsidered:

1. Are all the customers important? Is there any other way of servicing the less important ones? Through distributors, or internal sales staff, for instance.
2. Are the call frequencies the **minimum** necessary to win and hold the business? Could adequate contact be maintained with fewer visits and better use of the telephone?
3. Is the average daily call rate the best that can be achieved?

If the workload is still well over 1.00 after adjustments have been made, a solution to the problem must be found through discussion with sales management.

Time is a most valuable commodity, and is always in short supply. It is not unusual today for a sales call, even an abortive one, to cost a substantial amount of money.

The example which follows makes the procedure clear:

A salesperson has 230 customers and 50 prospective accounts. 25 of these customers need personal visits fortnightly, 75 of these customers need personal visits every 2 months, 130 of these customers need personal visits every 6 months.

The 50 prospective accounts will be visited at least twice in the year and on previous conversion rates 10 will be converted to a 2-monthly cycle.

The average daily call rate has, over the last 6 months, been 7 calls per day.

They anticipate having 210 days available for selling. Thus the calculation proceeds:

230 + 50 of which	25 ×	25 (fortnightly)	625
	75 ×	6 (2-monthly)	450
+ 10 prospects	×	6 (2 montly)	60
	130 ×	2 (6-monthly)	260
+ 40 prospects	×	2 (6-monlty)	80
			1475

$$\frac{1475}{7 \times 210} = \frac{1475}{1470} \qquad \text{Workload} = 1.003$$

Ask for any further questions before ending session.

TIME:

29

BACKGROUND NOTES

Managing the account mix

Every business needs customers. Yet existing customers not only have to be looked after, but may be the best prospects for the future. Time is taken up managing them, and then insufficient prospecting means ultimately too few customer, and a business in trouble. Yet, if prospecting becomes all consuming, and that takes too much time, then relationships with (and orders from) existing customers suffer – and again the business will be in trouble.

The answer has to be an effectively organised **balance**. Selling is as much to do with productivity as is production, where the term is more traditionally applied. So, that will be our starting point.

Sales productivity

Time is a resource just like, say, money. And no one ever seems to have enough of either. See how much, or rather how little, sales time is available. An examination of your own workload quickly makes the point. Calls are commodities which must be valued.

Amongst the implications, that for prospecting is clear. If you are only making, say, 800 calls a year it is very easy to omit prospecting calls – particularly if you like making them less than other kinds of call. Even if you resolve (or calculate) that, say, 10 per cent of calls should be prospecting ones, i.e. 80 calls, that is still **less** than 2 per week. And they will not all bring results.

The time spent on existing customers and prospects needs to be balanced. To avoid neglecting existing customers or failing to do justice to prospecting, the process that is involved in prospecting must be approached at every stage in a way likely to maximise the success rate.

You may wish to evolve your own definitions, and the stages vary from company to company, but broadly we need:

A number of

- **suspects**   (those worth investigating for potential follow-up)
- **prospects**   (those we decide are worth approaching)
- **agreements**   (those who respond to an initial approach and will agree a meeting or otherwise take things further)

In addition:

A number will become

- **following up** (necessitating more meetings/contracts/proposals etc.)

A number will become

customers

There is clearly a screening process likely here, in other words maybe ten suspects produce in time, one new customer.

The more favourable you can make this ratio the more productive you will be.

The next part of this workshop looks at ways of making the transitions from stage to stage more effective. The first question is: **How do we locate suspects?**, which we review next.

Session 3

A successful approach to prospecting

Ask where new customers come from – what are the sources?

List answers on the flipchart and highlight those sources salespeople can influence (e.g. personal observation rather than responses to direct mail).

Emphasise and explain key ones from those listed:

- personal observation
- past (dormant) customers
- suppliers
- trade associations
- exhibitions
- 'centres of influence'
- 'endless chain'

and others you may wish to feature:

Make a note of specific methodology that fits your operation (or against which targets are laid):

_____

_____

_____

_____

_____

_____

Having established that there can be regular sources of suspects:

Introduce the idea of 'screening'.

Explain that not all suspects have real potential. It is necessary to check them out to see whether or not they are real prospects.

Ask what information, or areas of information, can help select those with real potential.

LIst answers on the flipchart.

Highlight key categories to review in more detail:

Prospects may be selected by:

- *your products/services*
- *industry*
- *business activity*
- *marketing indicators*
- *competition*

Explain and discuss each section criteria progressively (ideally listing points on the flipchart as you go):

Your own 'product/service' indicators:

_____

_____

_____

_____

Your industry indicators:

_____

_____

_____

_____

(Here there is no point in being anything but company specific which – industries do you sell to and what are the priorities?)

Business activities:

_____

_____

_____

_____

Marketing criteria:

_____

_____

_____

_____

Competition criteria:

_____

_____

_____

_____

Option you may wish to discuss individual competitors, and what differentiates your company from them.

Ask with whom salespeople find customers make the most stated comparisons.

List those mentioned on the flipchart (try to put them in priority order). Take perhaps the most important two or three and review where any competitive difference exists (positive or negative).

Competitor 1	Competitor 2	Competitor 3

Make a note of any specific points you wish to add or focus on here:

_____

_____

Explain next the idea of selecting the best prospect. For this you may usefully devise a **prospect selector format** along the lines of the example that follows:

Prospect selector

To compare prospects, and help decide where time should be made available, you can use the form which appears next. This is designed to 'score' the *relative* merits of a number of prospects. You should:

● **write in prospect names** across the top of the first page

- **add any indicators** you believe are appropriate to your products or services
- In the space opposite an indicator, **fill in numeric value for each prospect** as follows:

  4 = Well-qualified   1 = Probably qualified

  3 = Qualified   0 = Not qualified or not applicable

  2 = Moderately qualified
- **add the columns** to obtain a subtotal for each prospect at the bottom of page 1
- **follow steps 1–4** for page 39
- **total the columns for each prospect**
- **determine those prospects that are best qualified**

This is where your subjectivity and experience come into play. There is **no absolute score** or cut-off point to determine best prospects. Compare the totals against each other and compare these prospects with others in your territory. If a prospect is obviously too low and not likely to make a good prospect you should probably eliminate that prospect from all future consideration.

Other prospects may not be worth pursuing at this time, but may become so in the future. Keep your evaluations of these prospects on file for later follow-on activities.

Explain:
- the concept of *relative merit*
- the procedure for use
- the scoring

If time allows you can complete – from available prospect information – one or more columns. Or issue a preprepared completed form.

Ask for any further questions before moving on to the next topic.

Summarise briefly and link to the next topic: having identified prospects we want to talk to, we have to make contact to try to arrange just that.

TIME:

PROSPECT SELECTOR

Page 1

4 = Well-qualified
3 = Qualified
2 = Moderately qualified
1 = Probably qualified
0 = Not qualified or not applicable

Prospect Name:

Indicator	
Prospect's type of business can best utilise my products/services	
The prospect's expenditures in my product/service area have been increasing	
Prospect has a major contract related to my product/service that is about to expire	
The prospect is not satisfied with existing service	
Prospect is in an industry for which my products/services are well-suited	
The prospect's business is expanding rapidly	
The prospect has added a major new product line	
The company has acquired another company	
The company has been taken over by another company	
The prospect invests relatively heavily in research and development	
The prospect has recently obtained a major contract	
The prospect is advertising widely for new personnel	
SUBTOTAL	

PROSPECT SELECTOR

Page 2

4 = Well-qualified
3 = Qualified
2 = Moderately qualified
1 = Probably qualified
0 = Not qualified or not applicable

Prospect Name:

Indicator	
There have been recent changes in management	
You have an inside salesman	
You have reference accounts that will have a significant impact on this project	
You have identified the decision maker, influences and recommenders	
You have no competition	
The benefits of your products/services are clearly superior to the competition	
Your price is better than the competition	
Your delivery schedule is better than the competition	
Your on-site customer support is better than the competition	
SUBTOTAL from PAGE 1	
TOTAL	

Note: this kind of format can, of course, be tailored to your own organisation's situation.

BACKGROUND NOTES

A successful approach to prospecting

Sources of potential contacts

Here the job is to find ways of locating, and going on locating names of new contacts (it helps if some of the methodology lends itself to a regular, systematic, approach).
Some examples:

- **personal observation**: e.g. new offices, factories that you see on your travels

- **scanning of trade (and other) press**: e.g. news of mergers, people changing jobs, company expansion

- **past (dormant) customers**: e.g. those – often many – in the files too long

- **suppliers**: e.g. those we buy from – can we sell to them?

- **trade associations**: e.g. publications, newsletters, events

- **exhibitions**: e.g. exhibitors and visitors

- **'centres of influence'**: e.g. bodies who can recommend potential customers rather than being one themselves

- **'endless chain' recommendation**: e.g. A recommends B who recommends C – (or at least does so when *asked*)

Some at least of these may be worth exploring in more detail and noting for future reference, indeed you may also be able to think of others – or variants – that are also useful to you .

Selecting the 'best' prospects

Now that you have a, replenishing, list of suspects you need to decide which to pursue.

A first screening rules out some of the most obvious factors. One may be far too small, another not on your territory (but needs passing on). Otherwise there is a need to define the 'best'. In some ways this is straightforward:

The best prospects are those likely to return the best results in terms of sales, bearing in mind the amount of time and effort you expend on them.

Ideally you want to work smarter, not harder, so you need some basis to sort the wheat from the chaff. The following dissects the process and makes sure you approach it systematically. Prospects can be selected by reference to:

- your products or services
- industry
- business activity
- marketing indicators
- competition

These are now dealt with in turn. They are not mutually exclusive and you need to watch for the mix most useful in your particular business.

Your product or service

Clearly your product or service will be more relevant to some businesses than others. To take an extreme example, a one-man business, issuing one or two invoices per month, is unlikely to be a good prospect for, say, invoicing systems.

Where the reverse is true you need a list of criteria which allow you to home in on a specific target group. Examples might include:

- size of the prospect company
- number of employees
- number of locations (offices, factors, distribution centres)
- level of sales volume

and, more specifically:

- prospect use/purchase level of your product
- prospect using more than one supplier

Industry

A straightforward method of selection is by industry. Either some industries are more likely to use your product/service than others, or your own expertise may make you more acceptable and more able to sell in one than another (e.g. an engineer in engineering companies.)

Examples are simply industrial classifications:

- the motor industry
- motor accessories
- publishing
- magazine publishing

and can be as general or specific as you wish, as well as reflecting your priorities i.e. some will probably be more important than others.

Business activities

Companies who are successful, growing, developing or 'on the move' often make better prospects than others which are not. Signs of this kind of business activity include:

- rapid expansion (visible in sales/market share/results declared)
- building new offices or factories
- launching new product(s)
- involvement in acquisition
- increasing (or heavy) investment in research and development
- securing a major order
- recruiting additional staff (job ads)

Marketing indicators

Here you are seeking factors that will make the whole process of marketing to a prospect – and hence the sales part of that – easier. For example:

- you already have a (named) contact
- you have other customers who will act as powerful, and appropriate, recommenders to them
- you have 'inside help', someone has moved perhaps from another company where they used – and liked – your product
- there is new management – a 'new broom' ready to explore new approaches – and suppliers

Competiton

Companies using one of your competitors may still be good prospects (at least you know they use your sort of product/service!) You may have an 'edge' if:

- your product/service benefits are clearly better
- your price is lower (or discount, credit or whatever)
- your delivery is faster or more reliable (or both)
- your after sales service/technical support/training back-up is better

You will surely have some points on which you beat competition.

Next, you need to consider a systematic method of assessing priorities (see prospect selector format, p. 38).

Session 4
....
Establishing contact and making appointments

START TIME:

Introduce the topic and:

Explain that there are two ways of making contact to be reviewed. Because letters often set the scene for a follow-up telephone call, the session will review letter-writing first.

LETTERS

The session can best be started with an exercise, but first:

Note: standards of persuasiveness in writing, in many companies, are lower – sometimes substantially lower – than with face-to-face contact. (It may be worth checking the kind of letters that are typically being used by your team. Some of these can even be used as examples later on.)

The prime cause is habit. Letters are written on 'automatic pilot' to a format fixed in the past. Too often they are bland, unimaginative, introspective and unlikely to make the right impact.

Because of this, a prime intention for this session is to change attitude – and persuade the group they *can* write much more effective letters if they *think* about it, and approach the task in a sales, rather than administrative, way.

The exercise that follows is undertaken at the start of the session so that the group will see, really see, how things are done presently.

EXERCISE

Ask people to draft a sales letter, one with the objective of interesting a prospect in meeting them to investigate your product/service in more detail.

They should ideally have a real (or typical) customer in mind. Allow 5–10 minutes for this and, once complete, leave the finished text on one side for the moment.

Explain the three key intentions of a sales letter.

Sales letters must:

- *command attention and generate interest*
- *be understood*
- *prompt action or commitment*

Check this is agreed and:

Ask for ideas of what more detailed content makes a letter persuasive and record suggestions on the flipchart:

List on flipchart, adding key points if necessary:

_____

_____

_____

_____

_____

_____

_____

Now return to letters exercise, and the text produced earlier.

Discuss a sample of what was done (depending on time) by asking:

● who has one that is really persuasive?

● who has one that starts really well? (openings tend to be weak)

● who is prepared to read their letter out loud?

Nominate someone if there are no volunteers, then pick more, two or three, to be read out before making comment.

Make a note of points you wish to include:

_____

_____

_____

_____

_____

_____

You can include letters you have gleaned from the files (keeping the writer anonymous if you wish) to provide additional examples

Discuss with the group the merits, or otherwise, of these. Highlight specific weaknesses, in terms of general points:

● introspection (every paragraph or thought starting with a thought comencing: we or I)

● ambiguous phraseology and in terms of specifics:

● muddled description of your product

This discussion session will, almost certainly, produce a consensus that letters are, potentially, a weak link. Next turn to two factors that aim them along the right lines:

i) Language

Ask questions as a prompt to going through the way in which language should be used in sales letters and:

List key points on the flipchart:

Persuasive written communication must be:

- *clear*
- *natural*
- *positive*
- *courteous*
- *efficient*
- *personal*
- *appreciative*
- *customer-orientated*

Then turn to:

ii) Letter structure

Explain the importance of structure, review the sequence, giving each a moment and referring back to the exercise letters.

Explain also that because letters are so important it is necessary to have a radical rethink about them, and because prevailing standards (in industry) are low, making them more effective is a real *opportunity* to stand out in the market.

Ask the group to turn back to the text they drafted earlier:

Review the content, asking are they sure – really sure – that it is the best way into the prospect, or is it too bland, formula, or simply insufficiently persuasive?

Ask them to redraft and spend some time discussing the new versions, rather as before, in the light of the overall coverage on this topic. (You might find a **checklist** – page 62 – along the lines of the example useful to help people review their drafts.)

Ask for any last questions about letters and then move on.

TIME:

TELEPHONE CONTACT

Introduce this topic by mentioning that, like letter-writing, telephoning can suffer from being taken for granted. You may like to introduce with a simple exercise that makes the point about the different, 'voice only', nature of telephone communication (for example: ask someone to explain to the group – not show – how to tie a neck tie. The results of such an exercise tend to speak for themselves).

Make a note of anything else you prefer:

_____

_____

_____

_____

_____

Explain the way the course will now cover the telephone call (and link to the telephone role play session).

The emphasis of this session is on making the call. It is, however, important to set the scene. Dealing with the next four topics allows you to do so without spending an undue time on the process. Each one includes a number of points, some of which should be dealt with by example/ discussion to involve the group.

i) Manner

Explain that how you came over is dependent on a combination of manner and voice/language:

List points such as:

On the telephone you must:
- speak more slowly
    than usual
- smile
- get the emphasis right
- ensure clarity
- be positive
- be concise
- avoid jargon
- be descriptive
- use gestures
- get the right tone
- be natural

And others if you wish:

_____

_____

_____

_____

_____

ii) Language

Next deal with language. There is, of course, a degree of overlap between language and manner. It is the combination which makes people say 'they come over well'.

List points such as:

> *Telephone language:*
>
> ● *be clear*
>
> *etc*

And others such as:

_____

_____

_____

_____

_____

It may be useful at this stage for everyone to hear their voice. The quickest way to do this, setting the scene for the role playing, is to ask each member of the group a question, passing a small recorder around the room so that it is in front of each person as they answer. The whole tape can then be played and any obvious factors (e.g. someone talking far too fast) can be reviewed.

iii) Two-way communication

Now make the point that the communication must be *two way*.

List such points as:

> Two way communication:
>
> - talk with people, not at them
> - remember to listen
> - clarify as you proceed
> - make notes
> - maintain two-way flow
> - concentrate
> - do not overreact
> - 'read between the lines'

And others if you wish:

_____

_____

_____

_____

_____

_____

_____

iv) Preparation

List key points to stress the importance of preparation:

> *Preparation:*
>
> - *objectives*
> - *right person*
> - *stages*
> - *decision*
> - *support/information*

And others if you wish:

_____

_____

_____

_____

_____

_____

(Link, briefly, to the **call planning format** on page 69 to which we return in the context of the role play.)

Introduce the topic of **getting through to the right person.**

Explain, with all the foregoing in mind, that getting through to the right person is a matter of 'strike rate'. We will not win them all, but the right approaches can make sure of a better 'strike rate'.

Ask what hazards to getting through exist and:

List them on the flipchart, discussing specific put-offs and seeking solutions to them. The following *examples* may be relevant (or there is space to note others).

Comments	*Possible responses*
'He's in a meeting.'	'Will he be available about three o'clock this afternoon?'
	'Could you suggest a good time for me to call him?'
'I don't know when she'll be in.'	'When does she generally arrive?'
	'Will she be in this afternoon?'
'What is this call about?'	'I want to talk to [name] about...'
	'I want to invite him to ...'
'You should really call ...'	'I agree it's important for me to also speak to [name], but it would be useful for [name of secretary's boss] to have an overall picture of what my company has to offer.'
'She does't talk to salesmen.'	'Then perhaps you can help me. I'd like to talk to your boss about her needs for... Can you tell me what her needs are in this area?'

List others:

_____

_____

_____

_____

_____

_____

Introduce now the specific process of making a structured call.

Explain (this may be recapping the basic sales structure if this has been dealt with separately in the context of face-to-face selling) and:

List the key elements of the appointment making call:

Appointment-making calls:

- *check you are through to the right person*
- *state your name and company*
- *give your reason for calling*
- *ask for relevant information*
- *give reasons for appointment*
- *talk of `working with' them*
- *mention/agree duration*
- *allow reasonable lead time*
- *offer alternative times*

Explain and discuss the key elements involved in actually tying down the appointment and **stress** that the call is *not* to sell the product/service but to fix the way forward.

One area where there may be demand for more detail is in how to handle objections or reasons not to proceed. The normal approaches utilised in face-to-face selling apply, but the following may help prompt discussion of ways of dealing with things on the telephone. (Remember answers always need matching to customers. They should reflect their feelings and attitudes, rather than being applied 'parrot-fashion'.) Your objective is to get the group to think about how to deploy arguments against objections, and to do so flexibly *not* just to learn standard reposts.

Objection	Possible response
'We're looking at the competition.'	'That's all the more reason for you to want to see everything that's available, so you can be assured of getting the service that best suits your particular needs. Our products have many unique features that might benefit you and your firm.'
'No need.'	'If I could demonstrate our services, you'd be in a better position to evaluate what you can accomplish with us. And should the need arise later, you'd be in possession of all the facts. That's why I called for an appointment.'
'I'm not interested.'	'I understand how you feel and I wouldn't expect you to be interested until you'd had the opportunity to see the many things we might be able to do for you. That's why I called for an appointment.'
'You'd be wasting your time.'	'I know there are many demands on your time, but I have enough faith in what my company can do for you to be glad to spend some time with you. Of course, there would be no obligation of any kind.'
'Just drop something in the mail.'	'I'd be glad to write to you about it. However, I'd like very much to drop in and bring you this information. Then I could explain a little more about the capabilities of the product and my company.'
'I'm too busy, call me next week.'	'I realise that you're very busy. That's why I called for an appointment that will fit into your schedule. I will only need a short time and I'm sure you'll consider the time well spent when you hear what you can accomplish with my product. Would _____ or _____ be better for you?' (Picking a time well ahead.)
	'What needs will you want to talk about when you have more time?'

Objection	Possible response
'Already know all about it.'	'Fine, then it will take me only a short time to bring you up to date on the many new features and benefits of our system.'
'How much does it cost?'	'Of course, the direct cost of any service is only part of the picture, We also need to consider implementation and service costs. I can give you an accurate cost after I understand your situation. For this reason, I'd like to get an appointment to discuss this more thoroughly with you.'
'My budget is exhausted.'	'Much of our business is based on reducing our customers' costs. I would like to show you how this is accomplished.'
'I'm not the person you should talk to.'	'Thank you for that advice. Could you tell me the name of the person I should speak to?'
'The head office makes those kinds of decision.'	'I see. It is important for me to speak to the right person. Who there should I invite to the demonstration?'
'We have our own.'	'I realise that. Many of our customers have, which just highlights the value they place on our company and the service we provide. That's what I'd like to talk to you about.'

List any further examples, or rephrase these in line with your own business:

_____

_____

_____

_____

_____

Ask for final questions on content to date.

Summarise briefly, and move on to set the scene for the *role playing* session.

BACKGROUND NOTES

Establishing contact and making appointments

There are two main ways of making contact with a prospect (other than knocking on their door unannounced or 'cold-calling' – which can be useful, but usually has limited application); these are by letter and by telephone. Or, of course, a combination of the two; usually a letter first, followed by a phone call.

As a general rule, it is often useful to write first if there has been no prior contact, and telephone if there has – as with a prospect responding to direct mail. In either case, if commitment is likely to be low initially it is worth considering an approach containing both letter and telephone; certainly you should not become fixated on any one methodology.

The fact that it may be complicated for someone out in the field to organise the letter, does *not* mean that it is less effective. The decision should revolve around what is best for the customer, rather than what is easier administratively.

As letters most often precede the phone call we will consider these first.

Letters

Consider first what makes a sales letter effective.

Overall it must:

- command attention and generate interest
- be understood
- prompt action or commitment

If it is to be *persuasive* it must also:

- be directed, specifically, at the recipient (not written for 'people like that')
- focus on the customer's needs (not yours)
- talk about needs satisfaction (benefits – what the product/service does for or means to the customer)

- use appropriate language
- have a well-chosen sequence and structure

Let us now consider the last two in more detail.

Language

Remember your intention is to prompt the customer to action rather than demonstrate your 'Oxford English'. We should write as much as we speak.

The following are some useful rules:

- **be clear**: make sure the message is straightforward and uncluttered by 'padding'. Use short words and phrases. Avoid jargon
- **be natural**: do not behave or project yourself differently just because it is in writing
- **be Positive**: in tone and emphasis (be helpful)
- **be courteous**: always
- **be efficient**: project the right image
- **be personal**: use 'I' – say what **you** will do
- **be appreciative**: 'Thank you' is a good phrase
- **be customer-orientated**: say 'You' more than 'I/We'

Structure

Any letter should proceed logically (from the customer's viewpoint) through its message. Very simply it will have:

- **an opening**: to gain attention, begin to build interest and lead into the main text
- **a middle**: the bulk of the content must hold, develop interest – talk benefits – remain customer-focused
- **an end**: perhaps summarising and certainly setting out what action or commitment logically follows

The *emphasis* of the message should be clear. There is no harm in using various graphic devices – <u>underlining</u>, *italics*, CAPITAL or **bold letters**, indenting etc. to create a letter that looks efficient, interesting and persuasive, as long as these things are not overdone.

Letters are often spoilt, and their effectiveness diluted, by being written on 'automatic pilot'. The pen was in gear, but not the brain. It is easy to find this happening. You get into a rut, you reiterate bland or inappropriate phrases that add nothing to the argument and, at worst, make the letter seem old-fashioned, unthinking or inefficient. For example:

- We respectfully acknowledge receipt of ...
- We have great pleasure in enclosing ... for your perusal ...
- We beg to advise ...
- The undersigned/the writer ...
- We are giving the matter every consideration ...
- If you have any queries ...
- We look forward to the favour of your instructions ...
- Assuring you of our best attention at all time ...

all give the wrong impression.

Most often the letter cannot sell the product or service; it must sell reasons why the customer should find out more, see it demonstrated, or have a meeting. The recipient must be clear what such reasons are from what you write.

Action

The ending – and the injunction to act – is perhaps worth another word.

You may want to take the next action. If so make sure this is clearly stated:

> 'I will plan to telephone in a few days to see how best we can progress matters.'

Otherwise, the letter needs a 'close', for example:

- **alternative close asking the customer**:
  - to telephone or write
  - telephone collect or use the reply paid envelope
  - send bankers' references or cash with order

- **concession close**:
  - 'we shall be able to let you have the current prices if you order now'
  - 'our normal delivery is two months, but since you are one of our best ...'

- **direct request**:
  - 'please clear the outstanding payment so we can continue shipments'
  - 'please post your order today so we can deliver this week'

In signing off do not automatically use 'Yours faithfully' for 'Dear Sir', and 'Yours sincerely' when the letter is addressed to an individual, but match to the tone of your general approach. Make sure your name is typed, and if – it will help the reader, add your position. Sign the letter yourself whenever possible, and consider letting your secretary use her own name rather than 'pp' if you are not able to sign.

If you use a postscript make sure it is a final benefit – an extra help to closing. Remember a 'PS' gets read, so do not regard it as just for omissions but consider how you can use it.

A checklist (see box) is useful both to check an existing letter for effectiveness and as an aid to composing a new one.

Note: Whilst wordprocessors are a great innovation, beware of inappropriate use of standard letters, paragraphs or even phrases. What makes a good letter is its appropriateness to a specific, individual, customer.

LETTER CHECKLIST

To _____   From _____

_____   _____

Objective of letter _____

_____

_____

Situation

What are my reader's needs or problems?

_____

_____

_____

What are my reader's likely objections ?

_____

_____

_____

How can my proposition meet his needs or solve
his problems? (Key benefits)

_____

_____

_____

How are the key benefits produced?

_____

_____

_____

Checkpoints

1 Is the letter written from the viewpoint of the person to whom it is addressed? YES NO

2 Will the opening secure favourable attention? YES NO

3 Does the letter cover all the information necessary to achieve its purpose? YES NO

4 Are the statements in logical order? YES NO

5 Are all parts of the proposition fully covered? YES NO

6 Does the letter avoid or overcome objections? YES NO

7 Is the request for response or action well expressed? YES NO

8 Is the general appearance of the letter good? YES NO

9 Is it grammatically correct? YES NO

10 Is it properly punctuated? YES NO

11 Is it logically paragraphed? YES NO

12 Is it free from trite and poorly chosen expressions? YES NO

13 Is it easy to read? YES NO

14 Can it be improved by shortening? YES NO

Telephone

Letters are a good, semi-permanent, reminder of your company, your product or service and of you. If they *earn* a reading they will increase a customer's perception and prompt action. You may find the customer on the telephone the day they receive your letter saying 'come and see me'. Or you may not.

In these circumstances the letter acts as a prompt. You can follow-up and find the customer is expecting you, waiting for you, or at least has experienced a spark of interest that is in mind as you make contact again. Usually such follow-up contact is by telephone. Sounds easy. Pick up the phone. Dial the number; and away you go. In fact, it seems deceptively easy.

There are numerous hazards. The customer may not be there. You may not be able to get past a secretary. They may take the call but have little time, or – worst of all – you cannot seem to explain precisely, clearly or quickly enough to create interest.

In addition, the telephone is different from many other kinds of communication (particularly the face-to-face meeting with which salespeople are usually most at ease), because it is 'voice only'. And, the problems of 'voice-only' communication are considerable, and in some cases prohibitive. Try describing to someone how to tie a neck tie for example – without any gestures or demonstration. It pays therefore to consider all the factors that can make vocal communication successful.

These are perhaps best reviewed in terms of how you use the telephone itself, how you come over, obtaining and using feedback, and planning.

The telephone itself

The telephone distorts the voice, exaggerating the rate of speech and heightening the tone. You must talk into the mouthpiece in a clear normal voice (if you are a woman, it helps to pitch the voice lower). It is surprising how many things can interfere with the simple process of talking directly into the mouthpiece: smoking; eating; trying to write, holding a file open at the correct page and holding the phone; sorting through for the correct change in a call box; allowing others in the office to interrupt or allowing a bad quality line to disrupt communication (it is better to phone back). All so obvious, yet so easy to get a little wrong, thus reducing the effectiveness of communication.

How you come over

Remember that on the phone you have to rely on your *voice* and *manner* in making an impression. None of the other factors of personality are perceptible. Here are some suggestions to help you:

Speak at a slightly slower rate than usual.

Speaking too rapidly makes it easier to be misunderstood and also mistrusted, although speaking too slowly can make the listener impatient or irritated.

Smile. Use a warm tone of voice.

Though a smile cannot be seen, it does change the tone of your voice. Make sure you sound pleasant, efficient and, perhaps most important, interested and enthusiastic about the conversation. Enthusiasm is contagious.

Get the emphasis right.

Make sure that you emphasise the parts of the communication that are important to the listener or for clarity. Only your voice can give the emphasis you want.

Ensure clarity.

Make sure you are heard, especially with names, numbers etc. It is easy to confuse S's and F's for instance or find 15 per cent taken to mean 50 per cent.

Be positive.

Have the courage of your convictions. Do not say: 'possibly', 'maybe', 'l think' or 'that could be'.

Be concise.

Ensure a continuous flow of information, but use short sentences, a logical sequence and take one thing at a time. Watch for and avoid the wordiness that creeps in when we need time to think, e.g. 'at this moment in time' (now), along the lines of' (like).

Avoid jargon.

Whether jargon is company (e.g. abbreviated description of a department name), industry (e.g. technical descriptions of products, processes), or general (e.g. phrases like 'good delivery'). At least check that the other person understands – they may not risk losing face by admitting you are being too technical for them, and a puzzled look will not be visible. Jargon can too easily become a prop to your self-confidence.

Be descriptive. Anything that conjures up images in the mind of the listener will stimulate additional responses from someone restricted to the single stimulus of voice.

Use gestures. Your style will come across in your position. There may even be certain kinds of call that you can make better standing up rather than at a desk, debt collection perhaps.

Get the tone right. Be friendly without being flippant. Be efficient, but **always** courteous.

Be natural. Be yourself. Avoid adopting a separate, contrived, telephone 'persona'.

Your intention as a salesperson is to prompt the customer to action. You should speak in a natural way that is absolutely clear. The following are some useful rules:

Be clear. Make sure the message is straightforward and uncluttered by 'padding'. Use short words and phrases. Avoid jargon.

Be natural. Do not behave or project yourself differently.

Be positive. Be helpful in tone and emphasis.

Be courteous. Always be courteous.

Be efficient. Project the right image.

Be personal. Use 'I' – say what **you** will do.'

Be appreciative. 'Thank you' is a good phrase.

(The language rules are not, unsurprisingly, so different from those relating to sales letters.)

Obtaining and using feedback

Talk with people, not at them. As a first step to encourage response, form a picture of your listener (or imagine them if you know them) and use this to remove the feeling of talking to a disembodied voice.

Remember to listen. Don't talk all the time. You cannot talk and listen simultaneously.

Clarify as you proceed. Ask questions, check back as you go willingly – it may appear impolite to ask later.

Take written notes. Note down anything, everything, that might be useful later in the conversation or at subsequent meetings. Get the whole picture and avoid the later reaction of being told 'but I said that earlier'. Do it as you proceed, not at the end of the call.

Maintain two-way flow. Do not interrupt, let them finish each point – but make sure, if they are talking at some length, that they know you are listening. Say 'Yes', 'That's right' to show you are still there.

Concentrate. Shut out distractions, interruptions and 'noises off'. It may be apparent to your listener if you are not concentrating on them – it will appear as lack of interest.

Do not overreact. It is easy to jump to conclusions or make assumptions about a person you cannot see – resist this temptation.

'Read between the lines'. Do not just listen to what is said but to what is meant. Make sure you catch any nuance, observe every reaction to what they are saying.

All the above will ensure the call flows more smoothly.

Preparation

Everything in selling starts with preparation. A telephone call is no exception. Just because it is brief, routine perhaps in the way it is viewed, it makes no difference. It will go better if some thought is applied first.

This does not mean a lengthy period of preparation, though certain calls may be well worth planning more formally, but it does mean the brain must *always* start working before the month! Planning will help you:

- overcome tension or nervousness
- improve your ability to think fast enough
- prevent side-tracking (or being side-tracked)
- make sure you talk from the listener's point of view
- assess your own effectiveness

and above all it will help you:

- to set clear and specific objectives designed to gain agreement and a commitment from the customer

Planning is necessary to make sure you direct or control the conversation without losing flexibility and reacting to customers accurately, without being led by them. It is rather like the helmsman of a sailing ship proceeding across an open sea, subject to the vagaries of wind and tide. He might take a number of courses. Having a theoretical ideal route to his destination in mind, however, will allow him to correct accordingly and keep on track.

Finally think about when and where you will make key calls – from a motorway call box? – a hotel? If they are important it is worth organising a timetable of when/where calls can be made. Plan to make difficult calls early and do not put them off – they will not get easier, rather the reverse.

The call planning format which follows is a useful basis for such planning.

CALL PLANNING FORMAT

Objectives	Methods
1 Specific objective(s) of call is to:	....
2 I plan to talk to whoever has the need, authority and money to make a buying decision related to my call objective:	....
3 My opening will be designed to:	....
4 My presentation will aim to:	....
5 I anticipate that the following objections will arise: (a) .... (b) .... (c)	....
6 I want to obtain the following decision(s) from the buyer: (a) .... (b)	....
7 To support my presentation I need the following information to hand:	....

Getting through to the right person

Perhaps one factor that puts some salespeople off making certain telephone calls is the difficulty of getting through, not just defeating the mechanical gremlins, but making direct contact with the decision maker. Switchboards and secretaries are often past masters at spotting, and refusing, anyone who is selling.

Prior research may have given you the name you want. If not always ask for the name first, and then to be put through, e.g.

Salesperson: 'May I have the name of your chief accountant?'
Operator: 'You mean Mr Morris?'

Then ask to speak to him. You may be put straight through and will know as he answers 'Morris here' that you have the right man – this avoids the need to check who he is as he answers. Operators and secretaries will often put a call through to a department or assistant first rather than the manager himself.

Alternatively more questioning may follow:

Operator: 'Who is calling him?'
Salesperson: 'Mr Roberts.'
(Your name is best said in full 'John Roberts' or even repeated 'Roberts – John Roberts'.)

Again you may be put through, particularly if the name is said confidently. The same applies to the question 'What company are you with?' You answer, confidently and without volunteering any extra information.

The really protective person will then ask 'What are you calling about?' Avoid cliché and the dishonest answer, e.g. 'a research survey', and describe briefly and comprehensively what you want to discuss (*not* what you want to sell him), e.g. 'I need to talk to him about computer stationery for the new EDP installations at your branches.'

The secretary/operator is unlikely to want to get involved in the detail of what may, by then, sound a little complicated and you should get through.

For regular or follow-up contacts the same principles apply, at least if there remains a chance they would rather not speak to you. It is useful to refer back to past events, e.g. 'I agreed with Mr Morris when I saw him last month I would call this week'. Only phrase it this way if it was agreed; alternatively say 'I said to Mr Morris ...' or, having written suggesting you call him on a particular day, 'Mr Morris is expecting to hear from me today'. (This can also be used as a follow-up to the right kind of phrase in a selling/prospecting letter.)

If the buyer is not there the secretary may offer to help or take a message. The most useful piece of information she can help you with is when the contact will be available to take a call. Ask 'Can I call back this afternoon?' or 'Will he be available tomorrow morning?' This saves time in further wasted calls and does mean you can tell the operator next time, 'I arranged with Mr Morris's secretary to call him about this time'.

Whatever kind of call you are making it is necessary to get through to the right person; what follows depends on the nature of the call and your objectives.

Making the call

If preparation has been adequate you can now make the call with confidence.

The stages and sequence you use during the call are important to its success. The actual sale will probably be made on, or after, a subsequent visit to the customer. The process now outlined therefore is designed for those circumstances, aiming at a commitment such as gaining agreement to a meeting and making a specific appointment.

1 An opening that:

- identifies yourself and your company
- establishes rapport
- gains interest.

2 Investigation – asking questions to ensure your message is based on facts.

3 Presenting your case.

4 Handling any objections.

5 Gaining/confirming the commitment you want.

6 Concluding the conversation.

Note: This parallels, and the following section encapsulates the technique stages of face-to-face selling (see *Ready Made Activities for Selling Skills*).

Each stage is now considered in outline:

Opening: Once you are through to the right person the next few seconds are vital to the success of the call. First impressions are always important; indeed you may not get a second chance. You can kill the conversation by starting with a long monologue about yourself, your products and your organisation.

The listener must not become defensive, so having introduced yourself and your company ('Good morning Mr Morris, I am James Roberts of Lingstones Containers'), using his name too if possible, you must then rapidly establish rapport and gain interest so that you can proceed smoothly with the call.

There are many ways of establishing rapport, e.g.

● make a friendly remark
● ask a 'yes' question
● tell him why you are calling him particularly
● flatter him (carefully)
● mention something you or your organisation have in common
● stimulate his pride
● acknowledge that he is busy

Gaining interest depends on talking early on about the customer, his needs, his problems – making him feel he has more to gain from allowing the conversation to continue than from letting it stop.

Not many products allow an introduction so powerful that interest is guaranteed, so find an alternative, e.g.

● tell him why he should listen
● tell him what he might lose/miss if he does not listen
● tell him what he individually can gain from the conversation

Best of all, link this rapidly with questioning designed to gain the facts you need. People are always pleased to talk about themselves and their situations, and you need to have sufficient information to present the right case.

Investigation means quite simply asking questions. But they must be the right kinds of question and of course you must listen to the answers and use the facts gained to guide your presentation. This process, particularly selecting which course to follow in light of the facts you unearth, must take place quickly. There is no place for hesitation or long pauses on the telephone.

What is needed are searching, open-ended questions, i.e. those that cannot be answered 'yes' or 'no'. Linking the next question to the previous answer will make the conversation flow naturally and prevent it sounding 'scripted'.

The more complex the sales situation the more important it is to dig deep, asking questions that progressively unearth the buyer's real needs. The four main types of question that can be used are:

1 Background questions, e.g. 'What's your unit cost per item?'

2 Problem question, e.g. 'Are unit costs a problem?'

3 Implications questions, e.g. 'What effect are high unit costs having on the rest of the business?'

4 Need questions, e.g. 'What would you like to happen so far as unit costs are concerned?'

Any initial reluctance to ask questions on the telephone will recede in light of experience – people really do respond positively to the opportunity to talk about their own situation.

Remember to make notes as the conversation proceeds and use the information to direct the call where appropriate.

Presenting your case

This must maintain initial interest, remain pertinent to the buyer's needs and give him enough information to agree with the commitment you want him to make.

Success at this stage is based largely on selling benefits, that is what the product or service does or means to the customer rather than what it is. A benefit describes the satisfaction derived from a feature or features of the product. For example, 'This car has a five-speed gear box' describes a feature. 'Additional fuel economy is possible because of the five-speed gear box' explains a benefit to the customer, and, provided it is based on the known fact that they will appreciate fuel economy, will be more persuasive.

Remember that unless you have set it up beforehand – perhaps by mailing your catalogue so you can say 'let's both look at page 10' – you have only the medium of your voice to rely on. This makes it even more important than at a sales meeting that everything you say is:

- descriptive
- stimulating
- expressive

For example, 'This equipment is very easy to use' only takes the customer so far. 'If your secretary can use a typewriter and a photocopier she will soon be able to manage this equipment' paints more of a picture, runs less danger of falling flat and will consequently have more impact.

Handling objections

Objections will always arise, even at this early stage of the sales process, and it is natural that they should. They may be a means by which the customer obtains more information, or just an excuse; they are nearly always an opportunity to progress matters further if you view them positively.

There are many kinds of objection. The following examples all assume that resistance is met in trying to make an appointment.

Personal objection. 'I don't have the time.' This may be true, but can also reflect the length of previous similar sales calls or experience of other salespeople's bad timekeeping.

Postponement. 'Why not put a brochure in the post as a first step?' This delays the meeting and suggests an alternative way of proceeding.

Price. 'It is too expensive' – perhaps the most common objection of all but it does not fault the product.

Product. 'This size of installation would not be right for us.' On the information to date they do not feel it would be useful to see you.

In handling objections, success depends on preparation, experience, knowing your market and products and on the way you respond.

On the telephone, with time pressing and the need to respond all too apparent, it is very easy to become defensive. Yet an 'ah, but' approach is the worst possible and will sound glib.

First acknowledge the comment, maybe just by saying 'Yes' or 'I see'. Pause (not too long) both for thought and to make sure an impression of consideration is received by the customer. Confirm your understanding of the nature of the objection. Then restate the objection as a question. This is a good technique. It not only clarifies, but objections need overcoming and questions just need answering, which is a much less emotive process. Answer in a way that takes the conversation back to benefits.

Gaining commitment

The 'close' is just as important in ending this kind of contact as it is in the sales interview and there is a danger in allowing what might be called a 'thank you' ending. The customer concludes by saying something like, 'Well, thank you very much, I have all the information I need for the moment, send me the literature and I will think about it'. He seems happy but there is no commitment. There is no alternative to asking for the commitment you want, but you have to take the initiative (this will follow naturally if you have really been directing the call). All the techniques of closing the sale apply whatever commitment you are after.

If or when you reach an agreement you must terminate the conversation politely.

Concluding the conversation

Do end on a note of thanks; that is the nature of the relationship. Reconfirm any final details and then stop. There is no harm in being first to say 'Goodbye' but you should be the last to put down the receiver. The customer may have thought of something else to say or ask. It can happen that if talk runs on unnecessarily the buyer may change his mind. Many a salesman who thought he had an agreement has found the buyer say something like 'You know, I've been thinking about that again whilst you were talking and I think a meeting may be a bit premature ...'

So hang up fast, but last.

Making appointments

The core of the call (perhaps even the entirety of the call) may concern making an appointment. This aspect needs specific thought and systematic approach.

Before you even dial the customer's number, you must have the following to hand:

- all customer information available to date, including any 'personal hints', which can help avoid gaffes such as the wrong pronounciation of the customer's name

- information on your availability (i.e. times that you can see a particular customer without disrupting your journey plan) and similar information on the customer (e.g. the record card for a known contact might state 'away at HQ on Friday', so do not ask for a Friday appointment)

- a checklist of the information you ideally want – other equipment being used by the customer, customer's preferences, size of company, etc.

The next step is again to get through to the right person. The best way to do this is to ask for who you want, confidently. If asked, give your name and/or your company name but no more. If you speak to a secretary, offer a suitable alternative, e.g. 'Can you make an appointment, or would you prefer that I speak to Mr Smith?' You will not always succeed, but such an approach will certainly help.

A structured approach with the buyer will have a greater chance of success than attempts at 'one-off' conversations. The following steps are advisable.

- Check that you are through to the right person.
- State your name and company.
- Give your reason for calling.
- Ask for any additional information that will be needed, or will be desirable at this stage.
- Give reasons for the appointment (rather than some other means of proceeding) in terms of benefits to the customer. The best reason is to find and mention something the customer will see, touch, have demonstrated – something that can only be satisfactorily carried out at a face-to-face meeting.
- Speak of the meeting as 'working with the customer' e.g. – 'If we meet we can go through the details together and make sure we come to the right solution'. This prevents them feeling they are allowing you to come 'and do something to them'.

- Mention the duration of the meeting. Honestly. It is no good pretending you only need ten minutes if you need an hour. At worst you may arrive and find they have only exactly the ten minutes you asked for on the telephone.

- Allow a reasonable lead time, for the customer. They are less likely to refuse an appointment for 7-10 days time than to refuse an appointment for tomorrow.

- Offer an alternative – 'Would 3.00 p.m. Thursday afternoon be suitable, or would you prefer the morning, say Wednesday morning?' – with the first option more precisely stated than the second.

Now and again resistance will be met, but you can then employ an objection-handling technique. The 'boomerang' technique is particularly useful for 'turning' an objection. For instance:

Buyer: 'It's not convenient – I haven't the time.'
Salesperson: 'It's because we know you're busy that we have prepared a special presentation, which will only take ten minutes [be honest], and it will give you the opportunity to inspect the product well in advance of its general release . . . we do expect demand to be very heavy.'

When you have got the buyer back on the track again, and sounding even tentatively agreeable, you can 'close' again as fast as is polite – just as if you were making a sales call, with the appointment as the objective.

If it is impossible to make an appointment, you can still get something from the situation by getting new information for the records. Having 'won' the conversation and 'negotiation' to that point, the buyer will often be in the frame of mind to allow you some concessions, and may be quite willing to give information about competitive products, his uses of that product range, names of others in his organisation you could contact etc.

Finally, consider the impact of just when an appointment is timed. First thing in the morning, last thing in the afternoon, or immediately after lunch, can help make the day far more productive. Additionally bear in mind that not everyone works the same day: one often hears sales people saying 'no one will see me before 10.00 a.m.' but for some customers 'first thing' means 8.15 a.m. and this may provide you with an uninterrupted hour (before the customer's switchboard opens) and a good start to his day.

If you are visiting the customer do ask about his location – a sentence or two may save you hours of searching. What about parking? Do they have a car park?

If they are visiting your office, factory or showroom, perhaps for a demonstration, make sure they know exactly how to find your premises – confirm this in writing (with a map if you have one) and inform others internally (including the receptionist) as necessary, making sure they know how important the visit is to the company.

Session 5

••

The appointment-making call role play

START TIME:

This exercise can be carried out with any number of people in the group, working in pairs. To provide sufficient examples, and avoid repetition, 8-10 people is, perhaps, ideal.

You will need to work out the time available for this session from the time it will take each pair to carry out a role play, and the amount of comment and discussion ensuing from the calls.

What you will need

You clearly need the ability to record the conversations. You can:

● hire (or purchase) telephone role playing equipment, consisting of linked telephones and recorder

● or, more simply, no more is necessary than two telephones (these need not even be connected, but it is important to a realistic feeling that participants hold a phone)

● a simple cassette recorder (or even dictating machine) which must have a tape counter

Then, if participants role play seated back to back (so that they cannot see each other's faces) they, and the group, can hear clearly and the recording will be satisfactory. See diagram on page 80.

This simple methodology can work perfectly well.

Note: (i) Such recording equipment will, when replayed, sound of a very similar quality to real telephone contact (i.e. less than perfect sound reproduction)

(ii) It is *always* advisable to carry out a short test recording and playback to ensure that all is working properly.

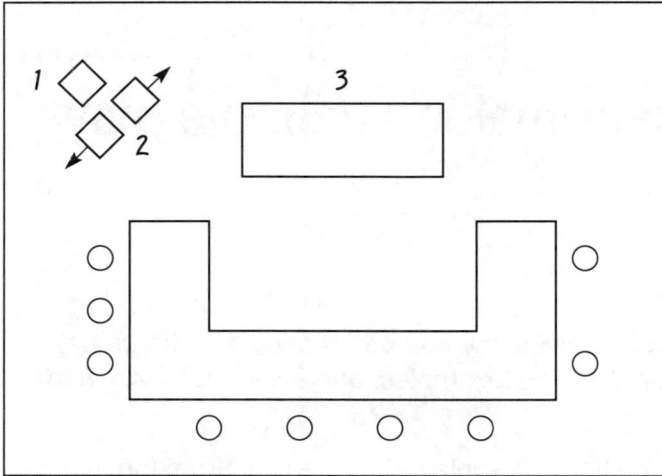

1 table with recorder and phones
2 two participants back to back
3 leader

Role play briefs

The intention is that the role play takes place around real prospecting situations, indeed it can even be a rehearsal for a real call.

You need, therefore, to select and write up the key essentials of such situations.

The salesperson's and prospect's role play briefs follow and provide the bare outline of what will be necessary.

It may be worth including references to:

● the nature and size of the prospect (i.e. organisation)

● whether it is a first or follow-up call

● something about the business potential

● the position, role and authority of the prospect (individual to be contacted)

List any others:

_____

_____

_____

_____

Such a brief can either be prepared by the leader or, time permitting, by those playing the sales role selecting a situation and briefing the buyer. The latter can be carried out before or during the session.

Once the role play is under way both parties should add improvised details as necessary.

Note: the role play should mirror real life, so the salesperson will *only* know about a prospect that they can ascertain by research; similarly, the prospect may know, by definition, very little about the caller. You may wish to document the details, see example brief.

SALESPERSON'S ROLE PLAY BRIEF

Objective: To secure an appointment, after completing the telephone call.

The call is between yourself and

Mr _____ , the _____

with _____Ltd

You have not made prior contact with Mr _____.
He is not expecting you and, although he knows of your company,
he knows very little of the detail of what you offer.

The role play opens with Mr_____'s telephone ringing.

Notes:

_____

_____

_____

_____

_____

_____

_____

_____

_____

_____

_____

_____

_____

CUSTOMER'S ROLE PLAY BRIEF

You are Mr _____ . You are the _____ with Ltd. The company's key operations include _____

_____ .

Your company's current needs/problems are _____

_____ .

Your overall budget is £ _____ . If possible you would like to have the solution to your need/problem solved, supplied and delivered within the next _____ weeks/months.

You are always interested in new potential suppliers.

The role play opens with your telephone ringing. You are not expecting the call and, although you know of the company, you know very little about them as yet.

Notes:

_____

_____

_____

_____

_____

_____

_____

_____

_____

_____

_____

How to organise the role play

1 **Explain** to the group that a number of appointment-making calls are going to be made.

2 **Divide** the group into pairs and explain that each pair will be asked to role play one of the calls. One person will be the salesperson and the other the prospect.

3 **Hand out** the role play briefs with each pair deciding which role they wish to play. You will need to work out the details and situation of the customer and their company and either fill in the briefs or let the participants fill them in to your instructions.

4 **Explain** how the role play will be conducted.

- **Say** that the main objective is to reinforce skill in managing, controlling and conducting such a call to produce a commitment.

- **Emphasise** that the exercise should be regarded as an opportunity to experiment and that it does not matter if mistakes are made in individual performances – it is more important to improve 'awareness' of how a good call is conducted so that improvements can be made in the future.

- **Explain** that after a few moments preparation each pair will conduct a call, whilst what is said is recorded.

- **Explain** that you will be recording the numbers on the cassette recorder for the start, finish and points of interest of each call (though, unlike role playing, say, a whole sales meeting, the short duration of calls normally allows the whole thing to be replayed).

Ask the group for any questions they may have about the procedure.

Because of the importance of the opening of the call – literally the key first few sentences – you may like to start with a 'silent role play'.

Ask all participants (or all those 'playing salespeople' to *write down* the exact words with which they will start the conversations once they have got through to the prospect, i.e. 'I am ...' the first statement of who they are, why they are calling, what they want.

Then get a number to read out what they have put, and:

Ask the group:

● How does it sound?
● Is its meaning clear?
● Is it delivered enthusiastically?
● Does it provide a good reason for the prospect to allow the call to continue?

Make a note of any additional questions:

_____

_____

_____

_____

_____

Discuss this and **emphasise** that, in real life, we only get one opportunity at this and, while it may be inappropriate to script it, everyone must be clear about the nature of a good starting point. (Some of the first written examples may well illustrate the need for a more precise approach.)

If you are going straight into the role-played calls then:

● **ask** the first participants to take their places and see if they have any final questions about what they have to do
● **give** the salesperson a minute or two to prepare (they can use the call planning format if they wish)

> This preparation can be done by 'thinking out loud' to involve the group – it may work best if, in this case, the prospect leaves the room for this brief discussion. They are, after all, aiming to try and respond spontaneously.

- **Ask** the participants to begin and switch on the recorder as you do so.

  Make sure that you are positioned so that you can see the recorder clearly. As well as recording the start and finish point of each interview, record the position of useful learning points.

- At the end of the call:

  Ask for initial impressions from the group, perhaps allowing the role play salesperson first comment.

- **Now play back** the call and stop (or invite others to request a stop) at suitable learning points and initiate discussion. Remember you are trying to build on strengths, as well as trying to highlight weakness. Overall the intention is to demonstrate better ways of working for the future.

- **Continue** this procedure through a series of calls by the group. You may alternate role play and comment (usually best) or record a number of calls consequentially before analysing them.

- At the end of this session:

  Ask for any final comments or observations, **summarise** any key lessons and thank and praise the group for all their contributions.

TIME:

Session 6
....
Planning the meeting

START TIME:

Introduce the session and:

Explain that there is an immediate need to link agreement to meet at the end of a call to *preparation* for that meeting, and that questions need to be asked about the situation to link to conducting a subsequent meeting effectively. Generally such questions as:

● Do we know all we need to know about the prospect?
● If not, what are the gaps?
● Can they be filled, by further research?
● Is information recorded?
● Is any liaison with others necessary?

Make a note of any more company-specific questions:

List such questions here:

_____

_____

_____

_____

Note: This session is a point at which you may wish to link coverage to the face-to-face skills area which logically start with preparation. It is here that this book links neatly to *Ready Made Activities for Sales Skills* for those using the two together. Otherwise the coverage here picks up at the point when, an initial sales meeting having been successful, it is necessary to consider how to start to manage the relationship on into the future to develop and extend the business opportunities. (This is picked up in Session 7.)

BACKGROUND NOTES

Planning the meeting

We have now reviewed the process of locating, investigating and approaching a prospect. If this is done systematically and persuasively you will get agreement to proceed further.

The next stage will vary, depending on the circumstances, the kind of business you are in, and, of course, on the customer.

Whatever form it takes, it is key. It has taken time, effort and money to get this far. Every call is expensive. It is important that it goes really well; which brings us back inevitably to **preparation**.

You will need to check that you are thoroughly prepared. Asking yourself the kind of questions which follow will quickly show whether there is more to be done:

- Do you know all you need to know about the prospect?
- Do you have all this information recorded for future use?
- Do you have the information available for use during the call?
- If you need to discuss the call with your manager, have you done so?
- Do you require additional resources for the call? e.g:
  - your manager
  - technical back-up
  - company literature
- Have you defined your strategy for the call? For instance, which factors are probably the most critical? Which ones will you try to pin down on the first call?
- Have you outlined and rehearsed what you will say and what questions you will ask?

Using the following checklist can help you organise for the sales call, making sure it is set up appropriately, and that you are clear how you are going to go about it.

SALES CALL CHECKLIST

1 Appointment

   Person: _____

   Position: _____

   Date/Time: _____

2 Objective of this meeting

   _____

   _____

3 Prospect benefit

   _____

   _____

   _____

   _____

4 Resources required

   _____ ☐
   _____ ☐
   _____ ☐
   _____ ☐

5 Outline specific benefits of your products/services

   _____

   _____

   _____

   _____

6 List questions under each key category to help you determine prospect's needs and your solutions

   _____

   _____

   _____

   _____

   _____

   _____

   _____

   _____

   _____

   _____

SALES CALL CHECKLIST (continued)

_____

8 Cost-justification data

_____

_____

_____

_____

_____

9 Follow-up activities

_____

_____

_____

_____

10 Notes

_____

_____

_____

7 Identify the decision-making process – the steps, the people, the timetable and whether adequate funds are available.

_____

_____

_____

_____

_____

_____

_____

Such a checklist (which can be amended, tailoring it to the specifics of your own situation) can be useful before, during and after the call. Each section of the form is now commented on in turn:

1 **Appointment:**   just the details of who and when.

2 **Objective:**   what exactly is this? Is it:

- to make a sale? (if so what)
- further information or qualification?
- to obtain an introduction to a decision maker
- to obtain agreement to proceed further:
  - put in a quotation/proposal
  - arrange a demonstration etc.

3 **Prospect benefit**:   based on information available to you and your contact with the prospect, determine how and why the prospect will benefit from the call. Why should the prospect see you?

4 **Resources required**:   place a slash (/) in the boxes opposite those company resources you require for the call. Make the slash an (X) once you have arranged for the resources. Use the blanks to fill in additional resources.

5 **Specific benefits**:   fill in this section before the call. Although you may not completely understand the prospect's needs, you do have some indication of what they probably are. Fill in any information you believe will be useful during the call.

6 **Key questions**:   this section consists of several groupings of questions that relate to needs and solutions. Answer these to the best of your ability before the call, and remember you may need to expand on them and other topic areas during the call.

7 **Decision-making process**:   ask questions to determine who will be involved in the decision process, what the decision criteria are and how the process works.

- Determine whether outside persons or influences will affect the decision (consultants, unions, government agencies or regulations).

- Determine if adequate funding is available (you may not be able to answer this until you've completed a visit); when it is available (this fiscal year, next fiscal year); whether or not the decision maker can commit the funds (does the request need to go before a board or to higher management).

  Do not be embarrassed to ask how the prospect intends to pay for your product/service.

- Determine when you might expect a decision.

8 **Cost justification**: use this section to record data that will help you cost justify your solution.

9 **Follow-up**: if things go well at the meeting and you discuss and obtain approval for the next steps, record them here.

10 **Notes**: provide space for additional notes.

A straightforward meeting may not, as mentioned earlier, be what happens. You may be involved immediately in a demonstration or a presentation. Presentations are increasingly common in many businesses, and must be well executed. The style of presentation being taken by the customers as indicative of quality, service and so on. Formal presentation involves its own set of techniques. So too do demonstrations, written proposals or any other additional stage involved (the detail of these is beyond our brief here, but is important in specific kinds of sale).

After the meeting

Assume you have identified a prospect, decided they are worth pursuing, made contact, obtained an agreement to meet, run an effective meeting (or demonstration or presentation) – then what next?

The answer may, of course, simply be to go back to the office and file the order. But there are other alternatives, the customer may postpone the decision, or want a quotation, proposal or whatever. Alternatively, the meeting may simply discover that they were not a real prospect after all and the matter is dropped.

Or – and this is always what you aim for– the order is secured and action then needs to be taken to secure intended future business.

Session 7

....

Maintaining and developing contact

START TIME:

Introduce the session and:

Explain the necessity to maintain good on-going contact and that this applies immediately and longer term.

i) Immediate follow-up

Explain the need for **persistent** follow-up and the psychological difficulty of doing this in the face of constant seeming rejection.

Ask participants for examples of what is said during typical follow-up telephone calls, say – the ubiquitous: 'He's in a meeting' and:

List such examples, adding any more you wish to introduce:

_____

_____

_____

_____

The lesson here is straightforward: do not give up: take such comments at face value (they will tend to say if they really want you to 'get lost'): ask and gain a commitment to when to contact if possible and keep in touch.

Discuss this in a way that shows that it is a common problem and seek examples of success that seemed never to be coming – 'after eighteen months they finally asked to see me again, I got an order at the next meeting and a good new customer thereafter' – to encourage persistence in an area where sales people often give up too quickly (though, realistically, you may wish to lay down some guidelines on when to cut losses so that time is not wasted on 'no hopers').

ii) Long-term contact and relationship-building

Explain the importance of this: – to sell anything you have to be remembered and you have to earn being remembered.

Introduce the concept of a range of contact methods and:

Ask for examples of ways to keep in touch:

- visit
- telephone (which tends to be overused or used unspecifically)
- fax and others.

Make a note of others or any required emphasis:

_____

_____

_____

_____

Discuss the need to ring the changes in terms of method.

Next:

Explain that there must be reason for such contact – a reason that customers will appreciate (it is easy to say why we want to make contact).

List and:

Discuss good and bad reasons *in customer terms*:

Good reasons	*Bad reasons*
To complete some information given	'I am in your area'

Make a note of others:

_____

_____

_____

This is a very useful area for an exchange of views, some of the group will have found ways to proceed that work well and which could be useful to others.

Introduce the concept of a systems-based approach here (the customer review form in the background notes on page 97).

Note: this area will need to be related to your own organisation – introducing actual documentation you use or plan to use – which might relate, in turn, to a specific proportion of accounts managed by participants (this is an aspect of the 80/20 rule). So:

Make a note of how you wish to deal with this:

_____

_____

_____

_____

_____

_____

_____

_____

_____

_____

_____

_____

EXERCISE

At this point you may want to ask participants to work out an example of a series of ongoing contacts for a real customer (perhaps to link with the introduction of a system and form to prompt this). If so you may like to:

● ask participants to select a customer (they may need the chosen customer file and/or record card to hand)

● allow them to work on this for a few minutes and then compare notes with a colleague, working in pairs to critique the chosen approach

● you can then take one, or more, as examples to discuss with all present.

Space is therefore left here to allow you to make additional **notes**:

_____

_____

_____

_____

_____

_____

_____

_____

Ask for any further questions on this topic before moving to a conclusion.

BACKGROUND NOTES

Maintaining and developing contact

Some customers present no problem in terms of the maintenance of contact. There is a prescribed system and they are seen once a month or whatever. Others demand constant decision as to how and how often they are contacted. As it is a basic rule in selling that to sell anything you first have to be remembered this is well worth planning. It is perhaps useful to consider ongoing contact in two stages: that of what is traditionally called follow-up, the keeping in touch about something specific but pending; and the longer term designed in part to prompt new initiatives.

Persistent follow-up

This is best described with an example. Imagine a sales call has been made. It has been successful as far as it goes but there is no order – yet. They want a quote, a proposal or just, as they say, 'to think about it'. It does not matter what precise stage is involved or comes next, the job is to keep in touch. When you telephone they are busy, out or unavailable. Most of us quickly become paranoid in such circumstances. It is awkward to know what to say or do next and easy to give up.

Be warned, some business goes, quite simply, to the most persistent. Whether you are calling to follow up a proposal or to fix a new meeting, it is perfectly possible that 'he's in a meeting' means exactly that. You have to persevere and keep making these calls. Check when he will be free, ask which day of the week is best, but keep the initiative and keep trying – by phone, fax or letter, in any way that will leave the chance of making progress open. If people really want to say 'no', they will. You must not become a nuisance, but it is much more likely that you will give up too soon and lose out because of it. Once a prospect has said 'yes' for the first time, then you can think about the strategy for longer term contact.

Longer term contact and relationship-building

It is vital that contact is maintained if customers are to see you as an ongoing contact. It is all too easy to be distracted by other (simpler?) matters and neglect such contact. Past a certain point it gets very much more difficult to re-establish.

A system to help plan and then ensure follow-up takes place is therefore essential. First, consider the various different actions you might take that provide 'keep-in-touch' opportunities. For example, you can:

- visit them (a face-to-face meeting might be best, but is an expensive way just to keep in touch, and not for every five minutes)
- telephone
- write
- write and send something (information, a newsletter, press release, press cuttings, an article reprint, advance notice of something, samples, ideas, literature etc.)
- introduce someone else (someone more technical, more senior)
- ask them something (advice, information, opinion) invite them to something (coffee, lunch, dinner, an event or exhibition)

You may well be able to think of more. With such possibilities in mind you need to implement action and here a simple form – linked to your diary – can help. Such a form can be tailored to your needs, but should record key details of the customer in the top half and a timed action plan lower down. An example (reproduced from *The Selling Edge*: Patrick Forsyth: Piatkus Books) is shown. This is not a record (though it becomes one), it is there to help specify the action to be taken in a way that flags what should happen next. It will also act as a reminder to ring the changes in terms of the method of contact, and can link to things that will perhaps be planned centrally, such as the dispatch of a newsletter to a customer list. Only by seeing the plan laid out in this way can the continuity easily be perceived. A linked entry in your diary will ensure the action happens at the right time and fine tuning can be carried out along the way if necessary; it is not a straightjacket.

CUSTOMER REVIEW FORM

Ref No: _____

To: _____   From: _____

Customer: _____

Address: _____

_____   Tel.No: _____

Contacts

1. Name _____   Position _____

2. Name _____   Position _____

Type of organisation _____

Buying record _____

_____

_____

Comments: _____

_____

Follow-up action

Date:

A reason for calling

You always need a good reason for calling. There is no such thing as the archetypal 'courtesy call'. It needs to be a good reason, not simply because there has been a long gap, worse still because 'I am in your area' (if they believe that you can go on to sell them Tower Bridge; but they will not). You should be able to give yourself a good reason for making contact in the customers' terms. Why will it make sense to them? Why will they welcome it?

Additionally, it needs to be appropriate to the relationship. It is not necessary to form a close friendship with every customer, though it helps to be on good terms with many and is pleasant to become friendly with some. Indeed it is important not to assume a deeper relationship than there is as this can, if you misjudge it, end up in you being seen as a time-waster as you constantly make contact 'just for a chat'. There is a fine line between the right and wrong relationship, and it may be different for every customer. As always what works best is strongly based on customer needs.

Cut your losses

Time is one of your most valuable resources. So, to end, consider whether there are limits to persistence. After all most acorns do not grow into giant oaks, they rot in the ground. Experience helps you spot the good ones, and sometimes to anticipate long-term prospects. We have all had instances of persevering over maybe a year or two of contacts and this paying off; but others come to nothing. Sometimes contacts should go on the back burner, they can be put on a mailing list, passed to a colleague and concentration can continue on other and better prospects. It is the balance here, between new and current prospects, customers and prospects, that makes the system work. Sometimes action is prompted well ahead. There is no reason why meetings cannot be scheduled months, or a year or more, ahead if that is what suits the customer. The best sales people are genuinely objective here: keep trying with appropriate contacts; deploy time away from the no-hopers towards better opportunities; keep prospecting to ensure 'new blood' for your total contact list; take a long view of follow-up and you will do better than those who fail to keep in touch or deploy a sufficient measure of persistence.

Session 8
Summary

START TIME:

Review, briefly, the main elements of the course perhaps referring back to the 'workshop map' diagram to pull things together.

Action plan

Ask the group to provide feedback on what they got out of the course and how they may change the way they do things in future. It may help if you prompt feedback by focusing selectively on key sections of the course. (You can always note others to return to later – at a subsequent sales meeting, for instance.)

List some of the key points made, and **ask participants** to make notes on action they will be taking.

Make a note of any points you particularly want to raise in summary here:

_____

_____

_____

_____

_____

_____

_____

_____

_____

Sales targets

As one of the key points for action, you may want to include gaining a commitment to a prospecting plan, and to some (or all) of the numbers and ratios involved becoming, formally or informally, targets. If so, this must be specific to the organisation.

Make a note of anything you decide to include here:

_____

_____

_____

_____

_____

Link forward to any further action or events (e.g. a revised system or target, a forthcoming sales meeting).

Make a note here of relevant points:

_____

_____

_____

_____

_____

_____

_____

Take any final questions and deal with any remaining administration, then all that remains is to:

● **thank** participants for what they have done and

● **close** the meeting, ending on a high note, an optimistic note as appropriate.

Make any final notes here:

_____

_____

_____

_____

_____

_____

_____

_____

_____

_____

_____

_____

_____

_____

_____

_____

_____

_____

_____

_____

_____

BACKGROUND NOTES

Summary

We have reviewed a key process; one that is crucial to the ongoing success of the business. Prospecting may be one of the least glamorous, and least liked, parts of the sales task. But it is important and, because some companies and some salespeople neglect it, it can give you a real edge in the marketplace.

The process is made up of a series of conversions, from suspect to prospect, from prospect to interested prospect prepared to meet, and so on. At each stage there is a success ratio – 'strike rate'. You will get some 'No's', and none of us like that, but the more carefully each stage is approached the better the ratio of success will be.

So,

● each stage must be handled appropriately and carefully

● each stage must be judged in customer terms not from an internal perspective (e.g. if a letter as well as a telephone call is appropriate, it must be done, and done well; not put off because of any administrative inconvenience)

● each stage must be followed through promptly (or after appropriate delay) or 'the moment may pass', and re-establishing contact becomes more difficult

Perhaps the most difficult thing in this area is commitment. It is often the case in companies not that things are done ineffectively or inefficiently, but that they are not done at all.

Whatever your record in the past, however much or little prospecting needs to be fitted in, what happens in future is ultimately down to you. Training can help, by explaining what needs to be done and how; role playing can provide practice, and management can, no doubt, cajole. But only you can make it work. At any particular time you must know:

● what proportion of your sales meetings should be with prospects

● how many approaches are necessary, allowing conversion rates, to achieve this number

● when they will be fitted into your future work pattern

A specific plan in this area might show, for example:

Number of names necessary
to produce prospect list   _____

Number of prospects to be
selected from the list   _____

Number of letters to be sent   _____

Number of telephone calls to
make   _____

Number of meetings to be held
as a result   _____

Ratio of meetings to orders
per week/month/year   _____

(and maybe other stages: e.g. proposals/quotations/presentations/
demonstrations)

and then, of course, you need to stick to it; and, in the longer term amend
the numbers in light of your strike rate and the company's objectives.

Equal in importance is the process of keeping in touch, of managing the
relationship and creating the sort of relationship that continues to
encourage and extend the business that results from it.

Nothing that has been said negates the importance of the face-to-face
selling job. Quite the reverse. Everything that has been reviewed in this
course is designed to increase the precision of what you can do in face-
to-face selling, to increase its effectiveness and overall strike rate.

There is no doubt that salespeople who take time over the preliminary
stages of the sale and the process of managing the relationship tend to
create an edge for themselves, and produce better results at the end of the
day.

Every salesperson enjoys signing up a new customer, however that
comes about. But it is doubly satisfying when you look back and know
you made it happen right down the line.

3

. . . .

TRAINING TECHNIQUES

Any training is dependent for its success on a number of factors. These include how well it relates to identified needs, how relevant it is to the real day-to-day job of participants, how participative it is, and more. The previous section, running chronologically through the workshop, was self-contained. Given both time to go through this and some, albeit small, degree of tailoring then the workshop that can be run from it can meet many of the criteria for successful and effective training. But one other factor is key: that is the way in which it is put over. The effectiveness of training messages, like humour, is dependent on 'the way you tell 'em'.

This section is not intended to be a complete run-down on training techniques, indeed your experience may well mean that you do not need this in any case. Rather it is designed to highlight key issues, as either an introduction or recap, and provide within this overall volume comment on everything that is necessary to run the session. It is arranged in four sections:

- presentational techniques
- techniques to prompt and handle participation
- the methodology of role-playing, which as has been said in the previous section can be of valuable assistance in developing sales skills
- the use of training films

This section is necessarily similar to that in *Ready Made Training Activities for Selling Skills*, however it is linked to the specific participative techniques recommended here and also provides general background for much that you might logically do to extend the topic of this book in training.

The four categories of training topic identified are now dealt with in turn:

PRESENTATIONAL TECHNIQUES

Whoever is putting across the workshop, how it is received will be dependent in part on the way it is presented. So presentation is important. But there is more to it than simply putting on a performance that is stimulating and sends people away with a warm glow as it were; you are seeking to ensure learning takes place and that practice, and thus results, change as a consequence. So the detail of how things are done is also important. This section is designed to highlight key factors which can be used to make your presentation more effective. If you see what you are to do as helping people to learn, in any case an excellent definition of training, then it makes sense to start this review with the group in mind and consider what helps people to learn.

Ensuring learning takes place

There are several classic ways of positively assisting this process:

● **Making the message relevant**. You need to keep the nature of the group in mind throughout, to make sure that what is said is in their language, relates to the real job they have to do and fits into their frame of reference. If the group see the training message as tailored to them, representing their situation and if, above all, they think it will help them do the job better or more easily – or both – then they will take an interest and learn. Having clear, stated objectives for the session and seeking participants' agreement to them is also important.

● **Use a logical order**. Any message is going to be easier to take on board if it is not a struggle to work out, so creating a good, clear and logical path through the content is important. The workshop material gives the material here a clear structure, and the working method ensures that logic comes over to delegates.

● **Use appropriate emphasis**. The message must prompt a concentration on it. This is helped by a number of things, such as varying the pace, but also by repetition. Never be afraid to repeat, albeit in a different way, the key elements of the content. It is the combination of methods – lecture, discussion, an exercise etc. – that can do this and really enhance the likelihood of participants retaining the essentials of the message.

With this in mind we can turn more directly to how to make the presentation work.

DO NOT ASSUME IT IS EASY

Any kind of communication can be, perhaps surprisingly, difficult. The difficulties stem from various factors, which, taking a positive view, means you must:

● vary the pace and keep up the interest as peoples' natural tendency is to let their minds wander rather than concentrate continuously

● work at achieving understanding by avoiding too much unfamiliar jargon, using visual aids to reinforce points, choosing your words carefully and fighting peoples' instinct to make judgments too soon by anticipating – often inaccurately – the totality of the message before it is even complete

● accept change is always seen as threatening until its usefulness is clear; if you advocate change make sure you explain both how it can be achieved and what good results will flow from it – for the members of the group

● accept also that there will be plenty of preconceived views and existing memories that act as filters to what you are saying; these may have to be aired and disposed of along the way if a new way is to replace them

● use feedback; the good presenter, and the good trainer, never stops for a second taking in how the group feels (formally by, for example, asking questions and informally by such methods as observation of expressions and reactions), and uses the information gleaned in this way to fine tune their approach as they go along

All these points speak of care being necessary and also flexibility.

Preparation

The difficulties mentioned above dictate the three key rules for successful presentation: prepare, prepare and prepare. It is that important. This does not necessarily imply a lengthy process – certainly the workshop set out in this book is specifically in a form that is designed to minimise preparation time – but whatever is done must be done thoroughly and systematically. There is no substitute for being truly familiar with the material in front of you, it will not only facilitate progress through the material but make you more confident and thus more able to fine tune, respond to questions and digress where appropriate and useful. A key part of preparation is creating guidelines that you can keep in front of you and which act as an effective prompt and make it easy to work through the content; the workshop material does just that and allows you to personalise as necessary.

The group

It may seem obvious but the session is not yours, it is the group's and all the focus of its preparation and delivery must reflect that. Ask yourself how it will be seen, does it reflect their needs, can it be used in their jobs? – any question that will enhance this focus. The presenter who prepares only to make it easier for themselves is not so likely to create a session that will work well for others.

A second point here is important and concerns how the group will see you. Any lesson is more likely to be taken on board coming from someone the group respect rather than from someone perceived as trying to 'teach their grandmother to suck eggs'. A well-prepared presentation, even a well-turned out presenter, makes a difference. Your knowledge and your professionalism can enhance learning. On the one hand you need to be perceived as the 'expert', at least to some degree; on the other hand you should talk about the 'opportunities *we* have to improve sales performance', rather than saying something that comes over as 'you people must get your act together'. As was stated earlier, training is helping people to learn.

The third point is to bear in mind that training is often perceived as a cure for weak performance. In order to create an atmosphere where training is welcomed by the group it is vital to ensure that the event is seen other than as criticism. Stating that you intend to build on strengths, listing successes, talking about *even better results*, all help this process. The need for sales training is often linked to external change. This may range from increased competition to new or revised customer expectations. Whatever the situation, even if there *are* some weaknesses of performance, you must start the exercise in a way that will make it more likely that people will listen and participate with an open mind.

Structure

After preparation, the greatest asset to good presentation is a sound structure. The workshop material has this built in, but the principles are worth reviewing and are gone through now in a way that takes in some of the other presentational 'tricks of the trade'.

The oldest maxim about communications is also one that offers good advice here: 'Tell 'em, tell 'em and tell 'em'. This means you should tell people what you are going to tell them (introduction), tell them (the main content) and then tell them what you have told them (summary). Whatever else you aim to do this one thought will act to keep you on track. However, it is not sufficient to have a structure, you must make sure it is visible and develop it as you go along, a process sometimes referred to as 'Signposting'. Frankly it is hardly possible to indulge in too much signposting as a session proceeds; it is a technique which allows the group to keep everything you say in context. They know the objectives, they know the structure and where you are in the sequence, how it fits in with what has been covered to date and what will come later, and can follow the thread that much more easily than with less information of this sort.

So, the overall structure is the classic: a beginning, a middle and an end. And each of these may have the same, thus the four main segments of the workshop which reflect the classic stages of the sale all need an internal structure. Consider the three in turn.

The beginning

It is a common cliché that you only get one chance to make a good first impression; but it is true. It is always right to get off to a good start. People make rapid judgements at the start of the session ('Am I going to like this? Will it be useful?'); a good start gets them in the right frame of mind and is also good for the presenter's confidence.

At the beginning of the whole session all the preliminaries need to be dealt with – the welcome, the administration and so on – and, at the same time, you must:

- gain the group's attention
- create (or begin to do so) the necessary rapport

The first can be helped by a striking start:

- asking a question (even a rhetorical one)
- using a quotation (to make a point in a memorable manner)
- telling a story, an anecdote, or a true, recent or memorable occurance
- stating a striking fact, a statistic say
- using something visual, a slide, a gesture to create impact

or something just downright intriguing to give the necessary impact.

The second is helped by an immediate display of empathy, a focus on the group and how they see things and sheer enthusiasm – always potentially infectious – for the event and the topic.

The middle

This is the core of the session, and must:

- review the content in detail
- ensure acceptance of the message
- maintain the attention of the group

The structure and 'signposting' referred to above will keep the content unfolding logically and smoothly. Sufficient examples and anecdotes will exemplify what is said, add credibility and make it live; they will also help maintain interest especially if the session is kept reasonably participative with questions and discussion acting as raisins in the bread. Make sure the words you use are sufficiently descriptive, for example you cannot say: 'This is like...' too often. As the details of the core content come through here, the visual aids used will help maintain concentration and concentrate memory (and have an additional advantage as an extra aid to the presenter's memory).

In research carried out on behalf of Kodak, it appears that people take in information in a way that is made up of:

Visual	55 per cent
Tone of voice	37 per cent
Words	8 per cent

Assuming this is correct, it is vital to create visual inputs for as much of the message as possible to increase the chances of more being taken in and remembered. It is because of this that this workshop suggests so much is put up on the flip chart which is the easiest form of visual aid likely to be available. Other methods make visuals – rather than words – easier to handle and the overhead projector (OHP) is the next most readily available device with this characteristic. So it is perhaps worth a short digression – checklist style – to set out some of the principles of using this ubiquitous but initially somewhat awkward piece of equipment.

USING AN OHP

Some care should be taken in using overhead projectors to begin with; they appear deceptively simple, but present inherent hazards to the unwary. The following hints may be useful:

- make sure the electric flex is out of the way (or taped to the floor); falling over it will improve neither training nor dignity
- make sure you have a spare bulb (and know how to change it) – though many machines contain a spare you can switch over to automatically – test both
- make sure it is positioned as you want; for example, on a stand or a table on which there is room for notes etc. Left-handed people will want it placed differently from right-handed people
- stand back and to the side of it; it is easy to obscure the view or the screen

---

- having made sure that the picture is in focus, look primarily at the machine and not at the screen; the machine's prime advantage is to keep you facing the front

- only use slides that have big enough typefaces or images and, if you plan to write on acetate, check that the size of your handwriting is appropriate

- switch off while changing slides, otherwise the group will see a jumbled image as one is removed and replaced by another

- if you want to project the image on a slide progressively you can cover the bottom part of the image with a sheet of paper (use paper that is not too thick and you will be able to see the image through it, although the covered portion will not project)

- for handwritten use, an acetate roll, rather than sheets, fitted running from the back of the machine to the front will minimise the amount of acetate used (it is expensive!)

- remember that when something new is shown, all attention goes, at least momentarily, to the slide; as concentration on what you are saying will be less, stop talking until this moment has passed

- it may be useful to add emphasis by highlighting certain things on slides as you go through them; if you slip the slide *under* a sheet or roll of acetate you can do so without marking the slide

- similarly, two slides shown together can add information (this may be done with overlays attached to the slide and folded across); alternatively, the second slide may have minimal information on it, with such things as a course title, session heading or company logo remaining in view throughout the whole, or part of, the session

If you want to point something out, this is most easily done by laying a small pointer (or pencil) on the projector. Extending pointers are (in my view) almost impossible to use without looking pretentious, and they risk you having to look over your shoulder.

The end

Whether the whole session or just of a segment of it, the final stage is an important one. There is a need to summarise and a need to end on a high note. The end is a pulling together; there should be no loose ends or unanswered questions, and, particularly, participants should leave confident that they have found something useful and, moreover, are well placed to implement what they have reviewed. The very end may consist of some sort of flourish. A quote, a punchy remark, an injunction to act, a little humour, perhaps, may all be appropriate on occasions. And the final word will often be a 'thank you': if the group have worked hard, paid attention and you feel action will follow then this is not all your doing, it is theirs too, so thanks are then certainly in order.

Summary (practising what I preach!)

Here the key elements have been touched on, but it is a large topic. Nothing is worse than being on your feet ill-prepared and struggling (except perhaps being a member of the group experiencing such a presentation!). Preparation is therefore the key. Preparation lays down the structure and makes the message intelligible, and that structure then helps you smoothly through the whole thing. Such a basis also gives confidence to the presenter. The whole rationale of this publication is to make the whole process of getting a session on sales technique together easier and more certain, but final preparation and implementation is with you and attention to detail pays dividends.

Two final thoughts, then the checklist (in the boxed paragraph) can act as summary: first, timing – stick scrupulously to the timings you work out and particularly make sure participants respect the timings laid down for breaks, exercises and so on. Anything else leads to some degree of chaos.

Secondly, training (unlike some other kinds of presentations) must be participative. This has to be accommodated in parallel into the smooth progress through the session and is the topic of the next section. So read on; if I said it will change your life, I would be finishing this section on a high note (though I might also be exaggerating).

CHECKLIST

Key principles of presentation

Overall have:

- clear objectives
- a sound, and stated, structure

- a focus on the audience's point of view
- the right tone of voice

and plan to earn a hearing not expect one.

The beginning

This must respect the audience and make it clear that you will be accurately directing your message at them and their needs.
Here you must:

- get off to a good start
- gain attention
- begin to build rapport
- make the group want to listen by starting to satisfy expectations, yet ensure they keep an open mind for what is to come
- position the speaker appropriately (e.g. as confident, expert, credible)
- state your theme, outline how you will go through it (structure) and make it clear this will suit the group (you may also feel it is appropriate to say how long you will take – if the timetable does not – and then stick to that time)

The middle

This is the longest section; it must:

- maintain and develop interest
- develop the case through a logical sequence of sub-themes and points
- illustrate as necessary, with descriptive language and visual aids

- overcome doubts and scepticisms, anticipate specific objections and deal with them and ensure that the building message is seen as of value to those listening

The end

There is a need to finish on a high note, maybe with a flourish. The concluding part of the presentation must:

- summarise and pull together the arguments
- stress benefits to the group
- make clear what action is now appropriate (and often actually ask for a commitment)
- finish on a memorable note

Throughout the presentation the **language** and **gestures** (how you appear and the animation with which you go about the task is just important as how you sound) used must be:

- clear
- natural
- positive
- courteous

and put the emphasis on the key points so that the overall impression is of out and out professionalism – your goal is to get your professional approach prompting people to think: 'This is the sort of person I could do business with' (or learn from).

Participipitative techniques

Presentation must be blended with participation to make any training session truly successful. Quite simply involvement makes it more likely that learning will take place and that practice will change as a result; as long ago as Aristotle – who said 'What we have to learn to do, we learn by doing' – this principle was understood.

This principle is now backed up by research and this shows clearly that learning is more likely if participation is involved, and that retention of what is put over is much more likely. Because of this the more you can create involvement in the session – especially if this takes the form of actually practising new techniques, the more likely it is that learning will be carried over and change real work practises for the better.

Prompting involvement can utilise a number of techniques, some as simple as asking a question, others more complex to set up, such as role playing which is very much part of the proceedings here and about which more guidance follows. Here we review some of the ways to get people involved.

Role playing is not always well conducted. It is important to address any concerns the group may have about it, perhaps based on prior, and poor, experience. Stressing the positive benefits, making it clear they will be well briefed and that it is an opportunity will help get over any misapprehensions. The key benefits should be seen as useful.

The process starts as soon as the session begins.

A number of factors within the overall introductions and initial formalities can be used to break the ice and begin to get people involved. It is often important for people to realise early on that they will not be able simply to sit and listen, they will be expected to contribute. Such initial initiatives include:

● issuing a simple instruction: 'May I ask you just to fill in the name card in front of you before we continue'

● asking for individuals to speak, perhaps to each other (where they do not all know each other): 'Introduce yourself to your immediate neighbour', for example, or: 'Ask the person next to you what they think is the most important objective today'

● using discussion of the brief for the course to get people talking: 'Now I have run through the objectives, can you think of anything else'

● the use of a formal 'ice-breaker' exercise

Once the session is under way, and exercises and role plays apart, much of the participation hangs round the use of questions – both fielding those asked and using questions to prompt discussion and comment. Avoid questions interfering with the smooth flow of the session, yet utilise them to best effect needs some care; the techniques are different for each kind of question usage. Each is taken in turn.

FIELDING QUESTIONS ASKED

Prompting questions

Some presentations may have a fairly open brief, and questions are very much for the audience to originate. Others may have a more specific brief and questions are needed to help achieve objectives. For example, if someone is presenting a plan to the board, they may want to see certain points raised, discussed and know that what they have said at a more formal stage has been clearly understood.

In such circumstances questions may well need to be prompted. The following sets out sufficient information for such purposes, though the principles involved can be utilised in simpler situations.

Put questions precisely

Questions must be put *precisely*. There is an apocryphal story of the question which asks people, 'Are you in favour of smoking whilst praying?', this does not sound very good, and most people will say 'No'. But ask 'Are you in favour of praying whilst smoking?', however, and most will say, 'Yes' (is there a time when one should not pray?). Yet both phrases concern the simultaneous carrying out of the two actions. The moral is to be careful to ask the question in the right way, or you may not obtain the answer you want.

Use open questions

Many questions are best phrased as open questions. These cannot be answered yes or no, and so are more likely to prompt discussion. They typically start what, why, where, who, how or can be neatly led into by asking people to:

describe…	explain…	discuss…
justify…	clarify…	illustrate…
outline…	verify…	define…
review…	compare…	critique…

Directing questions

The first decision is when to take questions. This can be seen as a compromise because:

- questions allowed at any time can disrupt the planned balance of presentation, unless you exercise control
- delaying questions to the very end can frustrate the group and give you a false sense of security that the earlier points have been accepted
- discouraging questions or leaving no time for them is poor training

You may therefore plan to take questions after each main point. Whatever you do, tell the group the rules; allow time in the presentation for the chosen methodology to work.

As you handle questions *from* the group you may find it useful to use the following techniques:

- acknowledge the question and questioner

- ensure, as necessary, that the question is heard and understood by the rest of the group.

- if in doubt as to what is meant, probe to clarify, and restate it back if necessary.

- give short informative answers whenever possible. Link to other parts of your message, as appropriate

If you opt, which you may want to, for questions at any time, remember it is perfectly acceptable to:

- hold them for a moment until you finish making a point

- delay them, saying you will come back to it, in context in, say, the next session. (Then you must remember. Make a note of both the point and who made it.)

- refuse them. Some may be irrelevant or likely to lead to too much of a digression, but be *careful* not to do this too often, to respect the questioner's feelings, and to explain why you are doing so

- and if you don't know the answer, you must say so. You can offer to find out, you can see if anyone else in the group knows, you can make a note of it for later, but if you attempt, unsuccessfully, to answer you lose credibility. No one, in fact, expects you to be omniscient, so do not worry about it: if you are well prepared it will not happen often in any case

Asking questions

The questions you ask can check understanding or prompt discussion and make the group think round a point, building their understanding. They will retain information better if there is an element of finding out involved in its acquisition rather than only 'being told'.

There are several ways of directing questions; they can be:

- **overhead questions**, put to the group generally, and useful for opening up a subject (if there is no response, then you can move on to the next method):
  'Right, what do you think the key issue here is? Anyone?'

- **overhead and then directed at an individual**, useful to make the whole group think before looking for an answer from one person:
  'Right, what do you think the key issues here are? Anyone? … John, what do you think?'

- **direct to individual**, useful for obtaining individual responses, testing for understanding:

  'John, what do you think … ?'

- **non-response rhetorical**, useful where you want to make a point to one or more persons in the group without concentrating on anyone in particular, or for raising a question you would expect to be in the group's mind and then answering it yourself:

  'What's the key issue? Well, perhaps it's …'

All these methods represent very controlled discussion, i.e. leader … team member … leader … another team member (or more), but … back to the leader. Two other types help to open up a discussion:

- **re-directed questions**, useful to make others in the group answer any individual's answer.

  'That's a good point, John. What do you think the answer is, Mary?'

- **developmental questioning**, where you take the answer to a previous question and move it around the audience, building on it:

  'Having established that, how about …?'

Whichever of the above is being used, certain principles should be borne in mind. For questioning to be effective, the following general method may be a useful guide to the kind of sequence that can be employed:

- **state the question clearly and concisely**. Questions should relate directly to the subject being discussed. Whenever possible they should require people to think, to draw on their past experiences, and relate them to the present circumstances

- **ask the question first to the group rather than to an individual**. If the question is directed to a single individual, others are off the hook and do not have to think about the answer. Direct, individual questions are more useful to break a general silence in the group, or to involve someone who is not actively participating in the discussion

- **after asking the question, pause**. Allow a few moments for the group to consider what the answer should be. Then …

- **ask a specific individual to answer**. The four-step process starts the entire group thinking because they never know who will be called on. Thus everyone has to consider each question you ask, and be ready to participate. Even those who are not called on are still involved

To be sure of using an effective questioning technique, there are some points which should be **avoided**, such as:

- **asking yes or no questions**. Participants can attempt to guess the answer (and may be right). These questions should not be used if you want participants to use their reasoning power and actively participate in the training

- **asking tricky questions**. Remember, your purpose is to train people, not to antagonise them or make them look bad. Difficult questions, yes. Tricky, no. Keep personalities and sarcasm out of your questions

- **asking unanswerable questions**. You want to provide knowledge, not confusion. Be sure that the knowledge and experience of your group are such that at least some participants can answer the questions you're asking. Never attempt to highlight ignorance by asking questions which the group can't handle. This is particularly true when you're trying to draw out a silent trainee and involve him. Be sure he can answer before you ask them the questions.

- **asking leading questions**. By leading questions, we mean ones in which the trainer indicates the preferred answer in advance: 'Mary, don't you agree that this new form will help solve the problem?' Such questions require little effort on the part of the participant, and little learning takes place. In addition, even if Mary didn't agree, she would probably be uncomfortable saying so. After all, that does not seem to be the answer you want

- **asking personal questions**. Personal questions are usually rather sensitive, even in one-to-one sessions. They are often inappropriate in a group session

- **repeating questions**. Don't make a practice of repeating the question for an inattentive person. Doing so simply encourages further inattention and wastes valuable time. Instead, ask someone else to respond. People will quickly learn that they have to listen

- **allowing group answers**. Unless written down (and then referred to around the group), questions that allow several members of the group to answer are not useful. First, everyone cannot talk at once. Second, with group answers a very few participants may well tend to dominate the session. And third, group answers allow the silent person to hide and not participate as they should.

Note: the one unbreakable rule all training sessions should have, clearly understood and adhered to, is:

ONLY ONE PERSON MAY TALK AT ONCE (and the leader must be the acknowledged referee and decide who has the floor at any particular moment).

Above all, let your questioning be natural. Ask because you want to know – because you want this information to be shared with the group. Never think of yourself as a quiz master with certain questions that must be asked whether or not they're timely. Let your manner convey your interest in the response you're going to get, and be sure that your interest is genuine. Forced, artifical enthusiasm will never fool a group.

No matter how effective your questioning technique may become, never consider yourself so clever that you can manipulate the participants. Manipulation is not its purpose. Instead, questioning should be used to promote and build genuine participation, not in bending the group to your will.

Finally, for questioning to be an effective instructional technique you must create the proper atmosphere in which it can flourish. For example, participants should never fear to give an incorrect answer. If wrong answers are discouraged, participants will respond more cautiously. People should never have the feeling that they are asking stupid questions. It cannot be over-emphasized that they should be encouraged to ask questions, at any time, about anything they do not understand.

Using exercises

Questions can prompt discussion, which is valuable in two ways:

- people like, and learn from, participation as a process
- the discussion may well be creative, casting new light on some aspect of the subject

but, people will learn still more from actually working as a task.

Exercises can be as short as a few minutes or as long as many hours. For the purposes of the present discussion, which relates primarily to short training sessions of perhaps three hours to three days, exercises can be conducted in several ways:

- **individually**: there is a place for participants individually working through an exercise: one benefit is that of letting people work at their own pace, and on their own situations or problems. Protracted individual exercises in a group situation *seem* to be inappropriate, and are therefore best kept short.
- **in pairs**: working in pairs gives some of the advantages of individual exercises, yet involves active participation. It is affected by room layout, and

works best when people are seated so that they can simply turn to their neighbours and go straight into an exercise without moving. (Additionally, an individual exercise can then be commented on, or developed in pairs.)

• **in syndicates**: working in syndicates takes somewhat longer, and may involve some moving about, but it is useful. There should not be too many in a group, 5–8 perhaps, and you can make it work best by suggesting that:

• a chairperson is promptly elected (or nominated) to control discussion and keep an eye on the time

• a secretary is chosen to keep notes of points agreed

• a presenter is chosen to report back to the main group

If each exercise has a different chairperson or presenter, everyone is given an active role as syndicate sessions progress, and tasks are spread round the group.

The ultimate form of exercise, particularly for training in interactive skills (and certainly here as we consider selling) is role-playing. This needs careful setting up, and is worth considering in more detail; this is done in the next section.

Note: solo exercises where delegates work on their own should not normally be allowed to become too time-consuming. Yet they may be necessary. Two that are suggested in the running guide in Section 2 are:

• composing a letter; this cannot really be done 'by committee' and it is important to demonstrate prevailing practice, habits and standards. If time allows this is no real problem, though it could be set as pre-course work so that participants are asked to draft something and bring it to the session. Such pre-course work can be used in a number of circumstances where solo work is necessary

• planning on-going contacts for an individual account. The point here is that it is, for each participant, their own account – the exercise acts as real practice or reheasral – and again elements of this may need organising ahead of the session (briefing as to the kind of account to select and instructions to bring records for it, for instance). In this case the solo part of the exercise links to subsequent work in pairs, which is another way of reducing the time taken with people working exclusively individually

---

Role-playing

Any training that attempts to develop an essentially interactive skill must make a firm link between theory and practice. This is perhaps particularly true of selling; its dynamic nature and the need to adapt, deploying techniques as appropriate to each situation, are key lessons to put over. Role playing is a well-proven way to exemplify the material presented and reviewed and, however participative the proceedings have been in other ways, it is well worth allowing time for such a session.

Role playing is a powerful technique, though it is not necessarily the easiest activity to organise if you are to obtain the best results from it. It needs preparation, thought and care and ideally draws on the field experience of the trainer (many would see it as difficult to train others in selling unless the leader has some personal experience of actually making sales calls). That said, its value can be considerable and it provides a safe opportunity to practise with no fear of upsetting any real customers, or losing business as a result. As such it may also be regarded as providing an opportunity to experiment in a way that might be regarded as risky in the real world.

Specifically, it provides:

- an opportunity for each individual to obtain feedback on their own performance (not least their own perception of performance)
- examples of common occurrences (problems, opportunities or whatever) for further group discussion
- a prompt to participants to think about and thus better understand the buyer's situation as usually some or all of them will take turns in acting out the buyer's role

Most usually, role playing will use video recording equipment to facilitate playback and discussion of each enacted situation. This is certainly best, and the following section is based largely on this premise, though there is no reason why you cannot handle things more simply. It can work with audio recording only, this is what is suggested for the role play of an appointment-seeking telephone call detailed in Session 5 (with specific details of the set up and equipment required). Alternatively it can be carried out live, without recording, yet still followed by review and discussion. This latter necessitates careful note-taking, and keeping the sessions short, or they go beyond anyone's ability to recall exactly what was said (and *exactly* what was said may be important). Now, back to the principles.

Before getting into more detail, it is worth considering the simplest form of role playing which is fundamentally just an informal enactment of a real life situation. For example, if you pose a question that leads into conversation: 'Imagine the buyer says ...' and you quote an example of what he might say, then you can ask: 'How would you reply?' If this last question is directed at a chosen individual participant, with an injunction for them to reply *verbatim*, then it will create a moment of conversation – this can be between yourself and one of the participants, or between two participants. Such a conversation can be continued for just a moment, or for a few minutes, after which the session returns to its normal format. This is role-playing; people are made to think about the topic, not in academic terms, but very much in its day-to-day application Yet there is no formality, none of the equipment, recording and playback more normally associated with role playing.

At the other end of the scale there is considerable formality, with all the panoply of equipment and recording which can be daunting. I have been involved in role playing which returns in four main sessions during the day to the same developing scenario, which even uses people from outside the course and the organisation (this, for example, in training in recruitment interviewing skills, where real interviews with actual candidates have been filmed – with the permission of the candidates – to assist in developing key skills); so elaborate forms are certainly possible, and can work well.

To return to the more routine, and start with the dangers, role playing can fail and, if it does, the cause probably lies among the following:

- over-awareness of the camera (or recorder)
- over-acting
- a belief that role playing means acting
- the difficulty of 'performing' in front of one's peers
- poor role play briefs
- weak management of the role play
- incomplete or unconstructive feedback after the role play
- those not role playing being given nothing to do

More positively, all role plays should be organised to achieve one or more of the following objectives:

- reproduce real life as closely as possible
- provide an opportunity to practise difficult situations

- provide an opportunity to practise new skills
- develop confidence
- enhance learning by building on success
- experiment with new approaches
- change negative habits/reinforce positive habits
- fix knowledge and an attitude of professionalism
- promote analytical skill through self-appraisal and observing others

The following details four different forms of role playing which, although these can be adapted, amended and used in a variety of different ways, make useful examples, and show how to make role playing work well and generate constructive feedback. Though I have described them in terms of video use, there is no reason why they should not be effective without this facility.

The 'classic' role-play

This is where two participants act out a situation to reinforce their sales skill. Assuming a clear objective, and the use of standard video equipment (i.e. camera/tripod, microphone, video recorder and TV monitor), the physical arrangements must be able to comfortably facilitate what needs to take place. The following examples show how this can be achieved. Though, of course, no one sequence of events should be followed slavishly, the following illustrates a typical approach.

- Issue the role play briefs to the two participants, and allow them time to plan their approaches. If either is playing himself this should be made clear. It is certainly less confusing if participants use their own names, whatever their roles.

- State the objective, and summarize the briefs for the observers.

- Issue any observation and feedback forms to the observers. (A specific sales training example appears in Figure 3.1.) Emphasise that theirs is an active role in the learning process.

- Introduce the camera operator (if one is used). Brief him on what he should capture on film, i.e. one participant's role, the other's reactions, or both.

- Indicate when you want the role play to end, i.e. after a certain time, or when a particular point in the content has been reached.

- Invite questions, ensuring that everyone knows what to do.

- Emphasise that a role play is a group learning exercise, not an opportunity to test one individual.

• Invite the two role players to take their places. (Layout needs some thought; examples appear in Figure 3.2, and of telehpone role play in Section 2, Session 5.)

• Take your seat near the video deck, and be prepared to note down the tape numbers of where key points occur during the exchanges.

• When the role play has finished:
  – thank the two participants and invite them to rejoin the group
  – ask the observers to complete their feedback notes
  – ask the two participants to write down their own impressions of their role play
  – allow the lead player to comment first, drawing in the other as appropriate
  – ask the observers to offer their initial impressions
  – offer your own initial impressions
  – play back the opening moments of the role play, using this as your cue to lead a discussion on particular details
  – ensure that the observers' feedback is constructive, and the participants are allowed to respond
  – use the video to highlight key points
  – at an appropriate point, draw the discussions to a close. Ask for final comments from the observers; invite final comments from the participants and then summarise

Your summary should be divided into distinct elements: thank and praise the participants; thank the observers; summarise the key learning points which first, directly affect the individual(s), and second, may apply to the group.

• Rewind the tape and prepare for the next role play.

The 'carousel' role play

This role play involves the situation being started by two participants and, at an appropriate point, being handed over to two others, who continue to act out the same scenario. It is thus a good way of involving more people in the group, more quickly.

Again a typical but not definitive sequence of events illustrates what is involved.

• Divide the complete process into suitable parts (e.g. a sales interview might be divided into the opening, establishing needs, presenting the product/

Figure 3.1 Observation and feedback form

Participants: Salesman _____   Customer_____

Role play objective: _____

	A+	A	B+	B
How well did the salesman listen to the customer?	☐	☐	☐	☐
How well did the salesman's replies satisfy the customer?	☐	☐	☐	☐
How clear and understandable were the salesman's questions?	☐	☐	☐	☐
How well did the salesman control the interview?	☐	☐	☐	☐
What was the salesman's level of product knowledge?	☐	☐	☐	☐
What was the salesman's level of competitor product knowledge?	☐	☐	☐	☐
How well did the salesman use his sales aids?	☐	☐	☐	☐
How well did the salesman spot and use opportunities to conclude the interview positively?	☐	☐	☐	☐

General impressions: _____

Recommendations: _____

Figure 3.2 Layout organisation using only the training room

Example layout 1

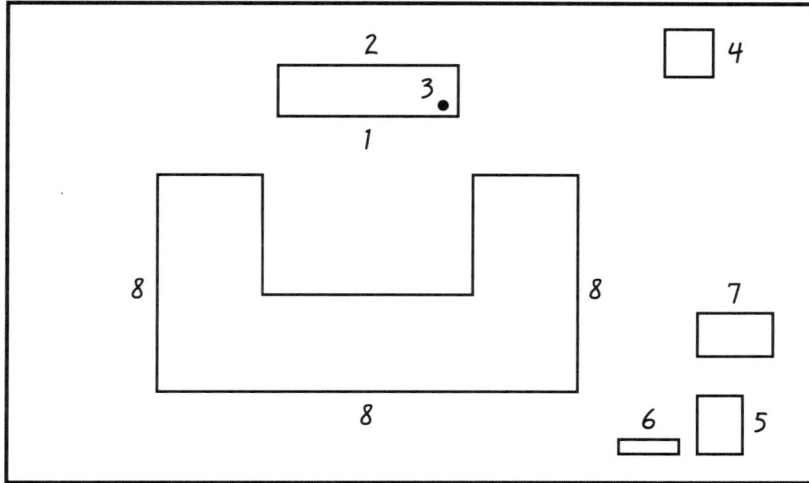

1 Player A 2 Player B 3 Table microphone 4 Camera 5 Video deck
6 Leader 7 Monitor (sound and vision off) 8 Observers

Example layout 2

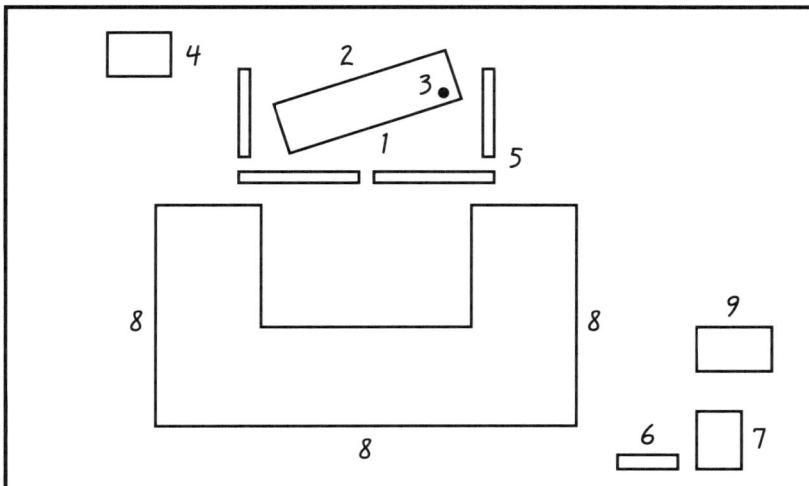

1 Player A 2 Player B 3 Table microphone 4 Camera 5 Screens
6 Leader 7 Video deck 8 Observers 9 Monitor (sound off, vision on)

service, handling objections, and gaining a commitment). Ensure that the group understands the basis for the split.

● Divide the group into pairs, and nominate who in each pair will play which role. However, do *not* indicate the phase which each pair will role play, not least so that everyone will concentrate throughout the proceedings.

● Distribute the carousel role play instructions (see example in Figure 3.3).

● Distribute any necessary role play briefs. (*Note*: all members of the group should be given the same two briefs, one for each of the roles.)

● Invite or nominate two participants to play the first interview phase.

● Begin the role play.

● At an appropriate point, stop the role play and either:
  (i) invite a second pair to continue from that point, or
  (ii) play back and take feedback comments, then invite a second pair to continue.

● When the complete scenario has been role played, lead a feedback discussion in the same way as for the 'classic' role play.

The 'silent' role play

Silent because the scenario is enacted in writing. This is clearly unsuited to anything lengthy, but is very valuable when there is great precision necessary (e.g. the brief moments when a prospecting salesperson introduces his company on the telephone; the succinct description of a key product benefit where the wording must be exactly right).

Again, a typical sequence of events illustrates the process:

● Divide the group into pairs, and brief them about their respective roles. Check that all is clear.

● Then a conversation is acted out and written down – word for word. This is done on the same sheet of paper – passed between the two – so that the developing conversation remains visible in its entirety.

● Once the exchanges are complete the whole conversation can be read out and discussed. (*Note*: this also works well with the leader playing one role and interrelating with individual members of the group; and also with syndicates discussing, and recording, a measured response.)

● There should be *no* talking between parties during the role play.

● The real learning will take place during and after the role play; it teaches the importance of thinking about, clearly expressing and logically structuring what

Figure 3.3 Carousel role playing instructions

OBJECTIVES

To reinforce skill at _____

To actively involve everyone.

1 One of our typical interviews has been broken down into its key phases:

   (i) _____   (iii) _____

   (ii) _____   (iv) _____

2 Each pair will role play one of these phases.

3 You all have a copy of the same two briefs, one for each role.

4 The first pair will role play the first interview phase. At an appropriate point their role play will be stopped and a second pair will be invited to continue the interview without losing its direction and building upon what has already been established. This pair will role play the second interview phase.

5 Again, at an appropriate point this role play will be stopped and a third pair will be invited to continue the same interview, also without losing direction and building upon the facts and agreements already established. Their task is to role play the third interview phase.

6 You must remain alert, listening and taking notes so that whenever it is your turn to take over you are able to maintain the interview momentum.

7 Throughout the interview you may introduce new information. However, if you do, this must:
   • not be designed to 'catch out' the other 'player'
   • not directly contradict whatever has already been established and agreed
   • sensibly reflect real life situations

8 The role plays will continue until a clear conclusion has been reached.

9 The leader may temporarily halt the role play between pairs either to play back the video recording or to summarise key agreements between the two parties.

---

you want to say. Seeing the actual words in black and white can be an object lesson in learning how to focus and clarify spoken presentation.

The 'triad' role play

As the name suggests, this involves three people participating in three roles during the role play session (e.g. a salesperson, a technical support specialist and the buyer; or a salesperson and two involved in the buying decision).

This can either work very like the 'classic' role play, or the third person can be an observer (but staying 'in character'); thus, the role play observer's task is to observe, then comment upon the two role play participants. (Essentially, he plays the leader's role for the moment.)

The remainder of the group have a dual task: to comment on the role play participants; and to watch and comment on how the observer conducts his feedback.

In the next role play, the observer moves into participant 'A's' seat, and A moves to the other side of the table and becomes 'B'. 'B' rejoins the group, and a new player takes over as observer (i.e. an element or carousel).

The leader's role is to orchestrate the action and learning, not forgetting that the emphases in this type of role playing are: the participants and the skills displayed, and the observer and his analysis and appraisal skills.

From the least formal format, mentioned earlier, to the more complex, role playing is an important tool of sales training. It should not, however, be underestimated in terms of the care and preparation it necessitates. If it moves off track, if it goes badly, then people are made to look inadequate which, understandably, they do not like. Providing participants are clear as to the brief, and understand the purpose of the exercise, and providing that the leader sets up the situation carefully and makes it a risk free experience, it can add to a training session to meaningful extent. Its greatest contribution is not in providing a test of individuals, but in creating discussion of examples and situations which the whole group can use, and from which approaches for the future can be constructed.

A final point

Finally in this section, there should be a recognition that not all the people in the group are the same. Everyone is an individual, everyone responds to the group situation differently; but you have to work with them all.

The use of training films

However stimulating the training, however much the participants are involved, participants may still be stimulated even more by greater variety of training methodology. And a classic way of providing variety in recent years has been the training film. There is a profusion of material available and good ones can do much more than provide variety.

Sales techniques, including the area of telephone contact used here as the main role play, are well covered so such films are worth a comment here. First the dangers: some films are promoted as being, or seem to be, self-contained; that is their topic can be put over solely by showing the film. This may be true of certain basic issues, but films will nearly always have a more pronounced effect if they are used as an integral part of a longer session.

How do they help training to be more effective? In several ways:

- first, film provides a different set of memories; through visualisation, character, humour or whatever they put a different complexion on the message and are a clear aid to retention
- they vary the pace
- they can introduce a topic, particularly to lead into discussion that extends its review
- they can act to summarise at the end of a session

or they can sometimes be used in segments, watching part of a film, pausing for comment or discussion, then returning to the film. However, they are intended to fit in, and whatever role they are intended to have, their effective use is dependent on having a clear objective not only for the course itself, but for the particular session of which the film is part. If you are clear on the point to be made and the result you hope to prompt, then, having considered whether a film will help, the next task is to select a suitable film. Most providers put out catalogues and it may be worth seeking to be listed on their mailing lists to help you keep up to date with exactly what is available.

There are two main types of film:

- **Right way/wrong way:** these may or may not have one continuing story line; either way they tend to start with incidents illustrating how *not* to go about the illustrated task. Then, in the second part of the film they set out examples of effective practice, and also comment on how this is done in clear steps. Often these can be suitable to use in parts.

● **Case studies**: these have a strong story line and the training message emerges from the incidents shown; again there is usually a clear summary or highlighting of key points. Usually these are best used by showing them without pause.

Both kinds, and most film providers/suppliers provide good back-up trainers guides in printed form. The best of these are excellent, and how helpful you find particular ones may usefully form part of a decision as to which film to use.

Films come in a variety of styles. Some are humorous, some to the point where there is a danger of humour overwhelming the message; others utilise a background that may or may not be appropriate for you (a large or small company, a technical or non-technical product, for instance). The main providers all produce comprehensive catalogues and offer a variety of ways of previewing their films – an unbreakable rule should be never to use any

---

USING FILMS

● View the chosen film in its entirety

● Make notes regarding:

  – significant scenes, points or dialogue that you may wish to quote or refer to after the film has been shown
  – key training points
  – additional points (sometimes necessitating 'reading between the lines')
  – prompts to discussion, and specific questions you will ask the group
  – names of characters or other details you may want to quote (it hardly positions you as an expert if you appear unfamiliar with the material)
  – any pause points you want to use when the film is shown to the group (during which you will use discussion, role play or other methods to exemplify the message)

● Read, and if useful annotate, the film 'trainers booklet' (even when you hire films these can usually be retained) which often contains more detail on the topic than appears in the film

● View the film again before using it on the session

---

film you have not seen through in its entirety and had time to integrate into the session. From this selection onwards it may make sense to adopt almost a checklist approach to how you use a film – see box.

Relating these comments back to the workshop described, a film or films (it is unlikely that you would want more than two within the content and extent of the material described) may well be useful to such a session. But it is by no means essential, and if film is used time must be taken for it to slot into the session and also, earlier, for its use to be prepared. The choice is yours. One final point: never use a film which does not really suit the session you aim to conduct, it will end up not simply failing to add to the proceedings but actually being a distraction.

Afterword

I know more than one editor who hates what he calls the 'untidy' afterword. But for the trainer, who has a – soundly based – predisposition to pull things together at the end rather than completing a list of points and finishing with the last one, they are a boon. Any communication to salespeople about what they do and how they go about it must not be totally technique led. True the techniques form, as it were, a foundation for what is done and should make it a sure foundation as they do so. But other characteristics of the process are important too.

First, selling is a complex social skill. Techniques are important, but so are systems approaches and the way in which everything that is done is fine tuned. Given the fundamentals, success comes through experience – practice; and such practice must do two things:

● it must deploy the techniques appropriately, customer by customer, day by day, meeting by meeting so as to maximise the chances of success in the short term

● it must take place with a certain awareness of how it is being done, and how well is all working, both to fine tune its precise application in an individual meeting to ensure the best chance of success.

Secondly, it must be accepted that the nature of selling is dynamic, the inescapable fact is that what works best will change over time. All sorts of pressures, competition, customer attitudes and so on change over time and affect how selling works. The best salespeople recognise this and work actively to keep themselves up to date. No one ever learns an infallible way to sell and can then simply apply it slavishly. Long term it can be the lack of this ongoing fine tuning of method that separates even the good salesperson from the best, with the less aware lagging behind.

Thus, at the end of the day, it is right for you to refer to what has been covered as fundamental techniques. There is an old saying that a person can either have, say, five years' experience or one year's experience multiplied by five. In selling, not only is the former the only way to ensure techniques are kept up to the mark, it is also surely what the people will want for themselves. Motivation, so important to the sales process, is surely not enhanced by believing that the job is essentially repetitive.

All this leads to the same conclusion, if you are looking for a note on which to end that links what has been done to the future, then perhaps the most valuable thoughts that you can leave with people are these:

- selling is, must be, dynamic

- performance can be maintained and improved in light of this by conscious practice

- any workshop provides the foundation (and should provide some immediate ideas and assistance), beyond that the only coach that is there to assist all the time are the individuals

- the best salespeople recognise this, act accordingly, and achieve better results – and greater job satisfaction – as a result

The future

Not only is selling a dynamic process, as has been said, it is also likely to increase in complexity in the future along with the way in which markets themselves develop. On the one hand there are always new – sometimes almost magical – approaches being promoted to assist the average salesperson become a star performer. Many of these are cosmetic or simply not credible. On the other hand the fundamental principles of selling – identifying needs, talking benefits, proving the claims that are made about the product or service and managing the customer relationships throughout the process as discussed here – are likely to remain important.

Beyond this there are other skills involved and other factors that dictate their relevance that are important for the future. A number of such are listed below, and may be worth keeping in mind or mentioning, particularly at the end of the training session to conclude with a look ahead:

- **the commercial environment**: selling is a front line activity and is bound to be subject to the prevailing economic and commercial pressures of the moment. Whether the market is in recession or a competitor has just launched a new product that makes selling yours more difficult, the sales approach has to include an appropriate response. There tends always to be something of this sort to actively consider and build into the way salespeople work

- **the marketing strategy**: selling does not exist in a corporate vacuum, it is part of the marketing and promotional mix. It must work in a way that is both effective and fits with the overall strategy of the organisation. For example, if the promotional platform stresses technical or service excellence then everything the salespeople do with customers must reflect that image. This too is a dynamic area and activity must always reflect current strategic issues

● **the buyers' attitude and expectations**: whoever the buyer is (and it may be more than one person) selling only works if it fits with their thinking and the way in which purchase decisions are really made. Sales activity must always observe and reflect this in a practical way

● **additional skills**: beyond the fundamental face-to-face skills, this book will help you tackle some of the next most important, those of account management and development. But that is not the end of it. Salespeople may have to excel in a number of other areas, these may include the ability to:

● sell 'on their feet' in formal presentations situations

● write more complex sales proposals/quotations than the letters dealt with here

● negotiate, which entails a set of skills separate from, yet linked to sales

These, and doubtless other points which could be made, are both illustrative of the key issues and representative of the way in which the selling job is going. I remember once telephoning a salesman who had been to see me and being told by his company's switchboard that he was out, coupled with the observation that: 'He's not often in the office, he's only a salesman'. Only? Anyone in selling can do with a great deal more support than that; but the problem remains. It is all too easy for people to be seen as 'only a salesman', indeed it can be possible that they begin to believe it themselves. Sales training should address issues that are based on the opposite view, that selling is a vital and complex task that can only be successfully done if it is professional. And salespeople that really believe not only that they are professional, but that it matters, will tend to produce better results than any that doubt it or see the whole process as merely routine.

If your training session builds motivation in this respect and acts to create a culture of professionalism as well as the knowledge and skill to do the job, it will be well worth the time it takes; if this publication helps you do both, it will also prove worthwhile.

READY MADE ACTIVITIES RESOURCE PACKS

Developing your Staff
Selling Skills
Customer Care Skills
Negotiation Skills
Presentation Skills
Financial Skills

In a high pressure environment you need to bring your team up to speed quickly and effectively. Waiting for the right course can waste time.

The *Ready Made Activities Resource Packs* give you access to material to develop your own skills and those of your staff in vital areas such as finance, negotiation and customer care.

You can see how simple it is to improve the skills of your staff and save your company thousands of pounds by completing the training yourself. It couldn't be easier with our unique new *Ready Made Activities Resource Pack* – and you don't have to be an expert or even have any training experience to use them!.

These special versions of the Ready Made Activities series come with the full endorsement of the Institute of Management and are available in a Ringbound Presentation Folder containing all the information you could need to present the new skills to your team.

All the *Ready Made Activities Resource Packs* come complete with
- Overhead Transparencies – impress your colleagues and your bosses with a professional presentation
- Free Video – reinforce the message or open your sessions with this ice-breaker
- Photocopiable Handouts – give your staff the key points of your presentation to take away and refer to again and again.

All this and more for only £120.00*

Available direct from Pitman Publishing
Telephone 071 379 7383 or fax 071 240 5771

*Price correct at time of going to press but is subject to change without notice

ORDER FORM

Simply complete and return to:
Professional Marketing Department, Pitman Publishing, 128 Long Acre, London, WC2E 9AN, UK
Telephone 071 379 7383 or fax on 071 240 5771

Quantity   *Total*

_____   **Developing your Staff Resource Pack** @ £120.00   _____

_____   **Selling Skills Resource Pack** @ £120.00   _____

_____   **Customer Care Skills Resource Pack** @ £120.00   _____

_____   **Negotiation Skills Resource Pack** @ £120.00   _____

_____   **Presentation Skills Resource Pack** @ £120.00   _____

_____   **Financial Skills Resource Pack** @ £120.00   _____

☐ I would like to join the free information service

Postage and packing please add:

UK   add £3.00 per order
Elsewhere in Europe   add £5.00 for the first pack, £3.00 per pack thereafter
Rest of World   add £9.00 for the first pack, £6.00 per pack thereafter

Payment (Please complete)

☐ Please charge my Access/Visa/Mastercard/ Barclaycard/Diners Club/American
   Express for £ _____ (total)

Card Number ☐☐☐☐☐☐☐☐☐☐☐☐☐☐☐☐   Expiry Date _____

Indicate both card billing and delivery address if these differ.

☐ Please invoice me at the address below for £ _____ (total)

☐ I enclose a cheque payable to Pitman Publishing for £ _____ (total)

Name _____   Position _____

Company _____

Address _____

_____   Postcode _____

Telephone number (in case of order query) _____

EC Customers please supply your VAT number _____